KV-386-027

The Principles of Teaching Economics

1-50

C

The Principles
of Teaching Economics

J. M. OLIVER

HEINEMANN EDUCATIONAL BOOKS

Heinemann Educational Books Ltd
LONDON EDINBURGH MELBOURNE AUCKLAND TORONTO
HONG KONG SINGAPORE KUALA LUMPUR
IBADAN NAIROBI JOHANNESBURG
NEW DELHI LUSAKA

ISBN 0 435 84525 x

Published by Heinemann Educational Books Ltd
48 Charles Street, London W1X 8AH
Printed Offset Litho and bound in Great Britain by
Cox & Wyman Ltd, London, Fakenham and Reading

Contents

For R.R.L.

Preface

This book is intended for my colleagues who teach economics and also for education students interested in teaching methods as they relate to economics. Little has been written about the teaching of economics compared with the Niagara of material on other disciplines, and what is written tends to be reports of surveys and experiment rather than a consideration of more fundamental issues. The book is therefore different in purpose from the existing colloquia and articles in the specialist journals.

I have not been concerned with specifying ideal syllabuses or describing novel teaching methods, and indeed my whole approach leads on to the conclusion that the first is a delusion and the second relatively unimportant. By discussing the nature of economics I have tried to provide an appropriate cast of mind with which students and teachers might analyse any particular teaching problem.

I have taken my illustrative material from all manner of levels and topics because I feel that the themes I have developed are of general applicability. I have not, however, been impertinent enough to explain a point and then illustrate it from every level in turn. Despite some provocation, I have sufficient confidence in my profession to know this to be unnecessary. The examples chosen are from that mainstream, Lipseyesque body of doctrine that is common to most GCE A level, HND/C courses, and to the early part of degree courses. Some of the discussion of curriculum problems and of objectives probably relates rather more to college courses than to school courses. This is a matter of acknowledging the world as it now is rather than a matter of principle.

The discussion is mostly in general terms, for the practical business of teaching lies in the particular and articulate application of principles. It is important not to tell the teacher what to do, but to discuss some of the criteria which might help him to decide what to do.

Some recent publications, chiefly by the AMA and the Economics Association, have discussed important day to day techniques, but this book is aimed at rather different needs. I hope it is a reflective discussion of the principles that might well underly practice.

This book has been a long time coming. It was born out of some years of teaching school, college and degree students of economics, and also students of education. It has been somewhat tempered by my experience as a chief examiner and an assessor – of which I have had more than my share. Other formative influences have been discussions with students and colleagues. It was W. H. Burston of the London Institute of Education who first taught me to ask at least some of the 'right' questions.

I am glad to thank my friends and colleagues, Jean Brown and Jennie Hardy-Smith, for typing the almost illegible original draft. I do, of course, take responsibility for all shortcomings.

J. M. OLIVER
February 1973

CHAPTER ONE   An Introduction

This slim volume is concerned with a number of related topics in the teaching of economics. It is not a work of research but rather of reflection, which I hope may lead others to reconsider some of the basic difficulties in the teaching of the subject.

The central theme, much underestimated in the published literature, is the impact of the nature of economics both on its educational role in general and on teaching methods in particular. Consideration of these relationships throws some helpful light on the arrangement and communication of material, use of visual aids, problem-solving, and the objectives of economics teaching. All these will be discussed in turn. They are not, of course, separate topics and the chapters are interdependent, not a series of distinct essays. This means that what is said about the goals of economics teaching cannot really be evaluated independently of the treatment of the nature of economics, and so on. It really does not matter in what order these topics are treated as none is complete without the others. There is some counterpart in the problem of topic sequence in the teaching of economics because full comprehension of any one matter needs some understanding of the whole system.

Economics is clearly the study of competing claims on limited resources – other, more modish, definitions are available. The methods of study are the techniques of deductive logic and also those of inductive reasoning. Most textbooks and courses emphasize the former against the latter. This is unfortunate since the inductive methods – which are largely statistical – are just as important. If a course concentrates on the deductive aspects then clearly it reaches rather different educational goals to one committed to all aspects of the subject. It means, if it is a degree course, that its graduates are virtually – or at least marginally – unemployable as economists; if it is a school course then the students have been given a distorted view of economics and a bogus notion of what it is, and what it can do.

A proper consideration of the nature of the subject leads us not only away from some of the more conventional views on syllabus content and objectives – problems to which we shall return – but also to wonder at some of the traditional enthusiasms for classroom techniques such as visual aids. If economics consists of deductive and inductive reasoning then visual aids can have only a small part to play because, quite simply, they do not involve deductive or statistical methods in any serious way. The same can be said of role-playing, factory visits and other favourites. This, too, is a row that must be re-hoed later on.

The scope, and so the limits, of the treatment are now clear. We are dealing with the nature of economics and then picking out some of the educational implications. While I am sure that these are fundamental problems there is very little in the way of grass roots advice that I can give. Indeed, this way of looking at economics teaching specifies the nature and so the shortcomings of some of the methods of enlivening material. Some teachers may feel that a number of these classroom techniques have been altogether too rudely dispatched; I have not deliberately tried to provoke, and it may simply be that some of these methods have been oversold in the past.

An important issue that helps to set the scene for a number of themes that will recur in this study is the relationship between economics and other subjects. I am not here concerned with empirical questions, which are much investigated, or whether students of economics and mathematics in general perform better in economics than students of economics and other subjects; but I am concerned with some of the other criteria by which we might assess the curriculum.

On the assumption that economics is a 'major' subject for the student, then economics – as the process of deductive reasoning applied to resource allocation problems – would be helped by the inclusion of two other kinds of subject in the curriculum. This is not to say that the exclusion of these subjects would make the teaching of economics in schools or colleges impossible and invalidate its claim to fulfil the three roles identified in Chapter 4. It is rather that if the economics student studies these subjects outside the time allocated to economics he will learn economics more effectively. There are two reasons for believing this. First, he will become more familiar with certain ways of thinking and thus probably better able to use them in economics.[1] Second, the economics teacher will not have to spend as much time on data and concepts which the student now learns elsewhere. In the extra time available he can raise the standard of the economics taught either by including more topics or by dealing with topics in greater depth.

In approaching this problem, we are going to say that some subjects fit well into the same curriculum as economics if they are complementary to it. For our purposes, 'complementary' subjects are ones which, studied together, give the student insights and an appreciation that could not have been gained from studying one subject alone and in depth. Subjects can help one another in this way either by means of technique or through content.

The two kinds of subject which would aid economics are those which offer a rigorous training in deductive reasoning and those which offer a different sort of analysis of similar problems. For instance, mathematics offers a training in deductive reasoning, and geography offers analysis of industrial location.

Presumably a rather general argument could be advanced in terms of any subject which calls for deductive reasoning such as logic, physics or astronomy. However, we need not linger with these more unlikely combinations of subjects except to say that in so far as they call for deductive reasoning they will be helpful to the economics student. It will not be true that they are more helpful the more they include deductive reasoning rather than, say, laboratory time. The important criterion is not so much deductive reasoning as such, but the areas to which it is applied. Thus the kind of deductive reasoning used in the problems of weighing a star in astronomy has, I believe, no direct counterpart in economics. Such reasoning might well be very formidable but it would be a 'transfer of learn-

[1] This does not quite carry the assumption of the 'transfer of learning' hypothesis. It is not saying that the study of one subject will help in the study of another subject, but that the practice of one kind of reasoning in a given subject could help the practice of the same kind of reasoning in a different subject.

ing' argument to conclude that therefore it would help the appreciation of economics, or to put it more generally, that studying a
difficult subject makes a person more intelligent in other activities.
But the kind of reasoning used in calculus – such as the study of the
effect of a change of A on B – does have direct counterparts in
economics (in the study of the effect of a change in production on
profits or of investment on employment).

Apart from this general comment on all subjects involving
deductive reasoning – that it is the kind of deductive reasoning
involved that is important – it is convenient now to concentrate on
mathematics. This is partly because mathematics illustrates the
general principles as well as any other subject and partly because, in
practice, it is the subject that students are most likely to study in
conjunction with economics.

The case for combining mathematics with economics has formidable support:

> To understand the place of mathematics in economics we need to consider
> the nature of economic theories. All economics theories have a common
> structure. First, a series of definitions define the terms used in the theory
> so that everyone knows the meaning to be attached to the words employed
> (e.g. by demand we mean the amounts people wish to buy at a series of
> alternate prices). Next there is laid down a series of behavioural assump-
> tions outlining postulates about the way the world behaves (e.g. the lower
> the price the more consumers wish to buy and the less producers wish to
> sell). Next a process of logical deduction is applied to discover what is
> implied by the behavioural postulates. At this stage the theorist learns
> what is implicit in his theories (e.g. a tax which shifts the supply curve
> of a competitive industry upwards by the amount of the tax will raise
> the market price by less than the amount of the tax). If the postulates are
> at all complex, some unsuspected and quite surprising results can often be
> obtained. The statements obtained at this stage are true if the postulates
> of the theory are true. As far as the world is concerned, they are to be
> taken as predictions, the empirical relevance of which cannot be estab-
> lished until a further stage of statistical testing has been undergone. [See
> 'Positive Economics', pp. 10–15.]

> It cannot be too strongly emphasized that in moving from assumptions
> to implications the only question is that of applying correctly the rules
> of logic. We wish to know what is and what is not implied by our
> assumptions, what must and what must not be true of the world if our
> assumptions correctly describe the world. For simple theories, verbal

analysis is sufficient and has the advantage of being generally understood although everything in this connection that can be done verbally can also be done mathematically. As our theories become even slightly complex, verbal and geometrical analysis begin to let us down; it becomes impossible to tell through verbal argument if a given statement is or is not implied by our assumptions. At this stage mathematical treatment becomes a necessity. The argument for the use of mathematics then is that it can do everything that verbal analysis can do for simple cases but, as our view of the world becomes more complex and subtle, mathematics provides the only satisfactory method of formulating and manipulating our theories. It is possible to argue that the world is so simple that mathematical analysis is unnecessary, but it is self-contradictory to hold that the world is so subtle and complex that the verbal forms of analysis are to be preferred to the mathematical.

Another great advantage of mathematical analysis is that it permits a formal treatment of theories in which behaviour relations are not assumed to hold exactly.[2] This indeterminancy in the relations might arise because we have left out factors which do have an important effect on the variable we are trying to explain, or because of an irreducible, unpredictable element of human free will. Contrary to popular belief, mathematical analaysis (involving behaviour relations with stochastic terms which have certain known characteristics) can handle such problems easily and effectively while the vague qualifications usually introduced into verbal analysis almost always have the effect of making us uncertain as to what is and what is not implied by the theory in question. Such a situation of uncertainty about exactly what our theories do imply is unsatisfactory from any point of view.[3]

[2] For example $D = f(p_e.p_1, \ldots, p_n, Y, \&)$ where D_e is the demand for eggs, $p_1 \ldots p_n$ are the prices of a few closely related goods, Y is consumer income and $\&$ stands for all other factors such as weather, consumer capriciousness, etc. that can cause the demand for eggs to vary. (The functional notation is merely a shorthand way of saying that the factor on the left depends on the factors on the right.)

[3] Some of the feeling against mathematics is no doubt caused by the undoubted excesses of some mathematical economists. Mathematics is a very powerful tool and thus can analyse the implications of very complex assumptions. This has sometimes led to a proliferation of more and more complex models without any concern for their actual or potential empirical relevance. This is a cogent argument for developing theories which are based on empirical observation; it is not an argument for abandoning a powerful tool for analysing the theories we do have. If misuse of a technique by some practitioners was sufficient reason for abandoning the use of a technique there would be few remaining techniques available in any field.

By and large I would say that the question of the value of mathematics in economics is no longer subject to serious debate amongst the younger generation of academic economists. In the United States where the bulk of the original work in the subject is now done, only the smallest minority of post-war economists would question the use of mathematics to handle the sort of theories we have been forced by the subtlety of the economic process to expound. In Britain there might be a larger number of dissenters but their number is dwindling and few of the academic economists trained in the last ten years would question this development; instead they would more often complain that, as victims of an outdated educational programme, they have been crippled for life by the absence of a good grounding in mathematics.[4]

The second modern trend to which I have referred is that associated with the concept of empirical relevance. Empirical relevance has always been taken as important criterion in economics. Indeed the giants of British economics such as Smith, Ricardo, Mill, Marshall and Keynes, were concerned to develop theories to interpret the world of their immediate experience. With the development of classical statistical analysis early in the twentieth century it became apparent that the economy was very often of sufficient complexity that a casual, impressionistic inspection of the data would not adequately establish the empirical relevance of a theory. The testing of theories on a more formal basis seems called for, and the Econometric Society was founded with considerable hope for the fruitfulness of such lines of research. For various reasons, one of the most important being that the theories were often cast in ways which made measurement of the variables and testing of predictions difficult if not impossible, results fell a great deal short of expectations. An important by-product of Keynes' General Theory was a great increase in the measurement of empirical magnitudes, since almost for the first time in the history of economics a theory was formulated in terms of variables with clear real-world counterparts having an obvious potential for measurement.[5]

Professor Lipsey is saying that mathematics is a useful tool for the analysis of all economic problems and practically indispensable for some. Our argument is now double-pronged. Mathematics is a useful subject for economists to study because directly mathematical

---

[4] 'For life' is not too strong a term because, although one can make good on some of the worst deficiencies by private study later in life, there is not a satisfactory substitute for a solid training during one's formative and most receptive years.

[5] R. G. Lipsey, 'Positive Economics in Relation to Some Current Trends', *Economics*, vol. 5, pt. 3 (No. 19), Spring 1964.

treatment can be used for economic analysis,[6] and sometimes *has* to be,[7] and secondly, it calls for similar types of reasoning to those used in verbal economics.

In terms of the educative claims made for economics by economists, mathematical analysis will help two of the roles claimed for it. It will support their intellectual rigour and academic expertise and also be of help vocationally as most of those who are employed as economists are employed in quantitative work. (The third role – that of 'cultural' background – does not seem to depend on assumptions about any curriculum relationship with mathematics.)

These comments that economics and mathematics should be studied in conjunction are in order as we are concerned with the principles of curriculum construction. In practice, they are a counsel of perfection. Neither university nor sixth-form students of economics can be assumed to have studied mathematics beyond O level. As a result, the economics teacher in secondary schools is forced to teach the odd mathematical concept to serve particular problems and the students are handicapped because they have a limited mathematical background. This emphasizes that the need is not really so much for the conventional A level mathematics syllabus as for some mathematics of a particular kind.[8] The most important mathematics would seem to be calculus, linear algebra, difference and differential equations. This is intended as a general remark of principle rather than as an operational comment on a conventional A level economics course. As these courses now operate it is not necessary to be expert in these mathematical topics, but such ability would undoubtedly help a student. This does not mean that non-mathematical economics is bankrupt but that it is weaker than the real thing and we do ourselves no good by pretending otherwise. At the moment, this is not a pressing problem with GCE candidates although it may well become so. Certainly, any experienced GCE examiner will be aware of the great advantages enjoyed by the

---

[6] E.g. In Chapter 3 it is shown that the profit-maximization conditions can be taught mathematically.

[7] Two examples are 'general equilibrium analysis' and the 'theory of the second best'.

[8] For details of the kind of mathematics see D. Bear, 'Mathematics and the Teaching of Economics' in K. G. Lumsden (ed.), *New Development in the Teaching of Economics* (Prentice-Hall, 1965.)

mathematically adroit candidate and these are even more pro-
nounced in college courses.

The economics teacher is sometimes driven to limit his syllabuses
to those problems for which verbal reasoning is sufficient. Although
this still makes available large and important tracts of economics it
remains true that the actual teaching of economics is poorer for the
non-mathematical straitjacket forced upon it and that the range of
the subject-matter is poorer also.

What subjects might be incorporated in the economics student's
curriculum because they involve a different analysis of the problems
he will meet in economics? An interesting case can be made out that
any sophisticated study of economics is well supported by a study of
academic sociology. Two reasons could be advanced. First that some
parts of traditional theory are gaining strength by drawing on sociological concepts.[9] Second, that some of the collections of resources
that economists analyse are, in fact, collections of human beings,
and for that reason have special problems open to sociological
explanation that other collections of resources, say machine tools,
do not have. However strongly this case might be argued in theory
or principle, at present and for the foreseeable future, sociology is
and will be outside the average sixth-form curriculum. There is
some growth in the study of sociology in the sixth form and this is
to be welcomed for the reasons just given, but college and university
courses offer greater scope for optimism – though in some cases it is
a nettle that has been grasped rather than an opportunity.

What other subjects might be included alongside economics in the
curriculum on grounds of their subject matter rather than the kinds
of explanation they use? The three obvious candidates are: geography, economic history and accountancy.

The study of geography could serve economics in a modest
capacity. The geographer addresses himself, among other things, to
explanations of the location of economic activity. In principle, his
explanation should presumably be identical but in practice because
of his different knowledge of concepts and data his explanation will
be somewhat differently orientated. The geographer and the

[9] E.g. R. M. Cyert and J. G. March, *A Behavioural Theory of the Firm*
(Prentice-Hall, 1964), and see N. Lee and H. Entwhistle, 'Economics Educa-
tion and Educational Theory' in N. Lee (ed.) *Teaching Economics* (Economics
Association, 1967), p. 54.

economist look at the same problem through different pairs of glasses.[10]

This gives rise to two possibilities. Either the student finds these different explanations helpful or he finds them confusing. If the latter is the case then this curriculum structure has generated a new, but solvable, teaching problem. Once the student is aware that it is not a question of incompetence of one of the staff but a question of gaining his own synthesis[11] by drawing strength from both disciplines, then this curriculum structure has served its purpose by making available to the student perception and understanding not normally available from one of the disciplines by itself.

The case for economic history teaching, apart from the fact that it is a form of history, is rather different. This is the economic analysis of past societies. How can this help the economic analysis of present societies? It may help in two ways. First, if the economic historian is using economist's concepts then the student simply gains more practice at using these intellectual techniques and this is likely to be beneficial.[12] Second, the study of past problems may provide data and illuminating parallels with modern problems. Thus a possibility exists that a study of the problems of economic growth can be facilitated by a study of, say, the British Industrial Revolution as an example of the growth process.

Although this is true there are perhaps as many difficulties as there are benefits. A superficial knowledge of the past may lead to the conclusion that the role of the innovating entrepreneur was crucial to eighteenth- and nineteenth-century economic growth and thus to the recommendation to nurture and support private enterprise in the present underdeveloped countries, despite their wholly different

[10] An interesting and similar problem has arisen in operations research. Those operations researchers in management and economic problems have been troubled by conceptual problems in using their techniques although exactly parallel problems have already been overcome by operational researchers in technology. (G. D. Davies and C. McCarthy, *Introduction to Technological Economics*, John Wiley, 1967.) Clearly there is still a great deal of bridging to be done here and a similar, but probably less urgent, problem exists between economics and geography.

[11] By reading, discussion and by special lessons from one, or simultaneously, from both staff members.

[12] Unless, of course, it precludes the study of some other discipline that might be even more helpful.

social structure, politics and culture. The irony is that a study of Russian economic history in the twentieth century could lead to precisely the opposite conclusion.

Now neither of these facile conclusions would be offered by a competent economic historian, which is to say that economic history is only of any real benefit if it is well done.

A study of accountancy would certainly help the economics student as there are a number of subjects the accountant has in common with the economist, and he certainly looks at them through different spectacles. Accountancy could be included in the sixth-form curriculum but this is an unlikely development at present. It is, therefore, likely that the economist needs to find some room for accounting concepts in his syllabus to help him in teaching Social Accounting, Balance of Payments and some of the problems of the firm. Again the position is different in college courses.

All the foregoing discussion has carried the implicit assumption that the curriculum within which economics is studied is constructed by finding subjects that are helpful to economics, that is that are complementary to it. A quite different assumption would be to construct a curriculum by finding contrasting subjects.

Upon what grounds might a curriculum be deliberately constructed that bracketed together economics and a quite disparate subject such as music or poetry? The most likely reason is that this would help to produce an 'educated' person. This gives rise to a problem well outside a study of the problems of economics teaching, but a few comments seem to be in order.

First, studying less economics and more of a disparate subject must make the student less of an economist. Any reply that nevertheless it makes him better educated carries the ironical implication that to be a good economist is to be poorly educated! This would take a great deal of proving. Second, and more serious, if the reply is that such a curriculum provides a 'better' education then the burden of proof is on those who define a good education as a wide one. It would be difficult to demonstrate that such a definition is a proper one. Third, even if it could be so shown it would still need to be demonstrated that there is a causal relationship between a curriculum and a person's interests. That is even if a person of wide interests is more educated it would have to be shown that a wide curriculum provides wide interests. This too would be difficult; many a person who has genuinely wide interests including, say, history, has studied little academic history and some people who did study history in some depth never open a history book now. It may be a sensible presumption that a widely based curriculum produces a wide range of interests but there is certainly no necessary relationship. There are certainly other possible sources of a wide range of interests, such as the influence of family and friends. All we can say is that a wide curriculum widens the options available to a student in the development of his interests.

No more need be said in the present context as the economist can bring special expertise to the structure of a curriculum based on the assumption of finding complementary subjects to economics, but the identification in detail of the appropriate contrasting subject seems a slippery enterprise as far as principles are concerned. We are concerned with the nature of economics and the problems of teaching it – rather than the problems of having been taught too much of it and so being in need of contrasting subjects, or of being taught some other subject and needing economics as a contrast.

The theme of all this is really that the principles of curriculum structure are to be found in the nature of the subject and the purpose and level at which economics is being taught. The exact subjects which relate to economics and the specific syllabus content will vary with the particular vineyard in which the teacher toils. It is both boring and unnecessary to detail the manner in which these considerations would show themselves in different courses – school general studies, O and A level, HND/C and in degree courses ranging from all manner of multi-disciplinary to single-honours.

One point might, however, be made here – and that is that courses which contain minimal mathematics are limited in their correspondence to real economics. The question we have to face is: are the modifications thus imposed in fact distortions? Such courses cannot meet all the objectives which we might set for a proper economics course – what objectives can they meet and is 'general' economics worth doing at all?

The numbers now studying economics at all levels make these narcissistic questions rather pressing. Economics is now in a dominant position in schools, colleges and universities, but economists, of all people, know that nothing is sacred. We must fulfil the claims we make for the value of our subject – these are discussed later – or go the way of classics which once held an analogous position.

The teaching of economics might be thought to be of interest as a matter of principle to a rather specialist group but it is also of some practical and general importance due to the remarkable increase in the numbers of students of economics in recent years. A few figures will suffice to make the point.[13] The percentage change in CSE and GCE O level passes between 1960 and 1970 was 296·3 per cent which was the highest for any subject and has to be set against a total increase of 42·9 per cent. The figures for A level passes for the same period were 361·0 per cent against a total of 107·2 per cent. There were over 33 000 candidates in economics for CSE and GCE O level and over 25 000 A level candidates by 1970. If we look at the courses in the Further Education sector that contain economics, by 1970 there were 3 739 candidates for HND; 3 570 for HNC; 41 769 for advanced courses in social, administrative and business studies; 22 502 in social, administrative and business studies for professional courses; 7 960 for OND; 13 859 for ONC. No doubt some students appear in more than one category and professional courses in particular do not normally have economics in every year. Nevertheless, these are formidable figures and a tribute to the teachers who coped with these demands despite the fact that many took only subsidiary economics in their degrees and despite the scarcity of economics teaching methods courses in colleges and Institutes of Education. It is a credit also to the Economics Association which is the main professional body in this area.

[13] Department of Education and Science, *Statistics of Education, 1970* (HMSO, 1972). Vol. 2, pp. 81–2; Vol. 3, pp. 28–9, 33–4, 36, 38, 42–5.

CHAPTER TWO   The Nature of
Economics

There has been an embarrassing difference between the rigour and elegance with which economists have thought and written about economics and that with which they have thought and written about the teaching of economics. There is much to be proud of in modern professional economics but much less in what is known and published about either economics teaching methods, or the educational role of economics. One particular facet which has had little attention is the nature of economics and how that might affect both teaching methods and the educational functions that the subject is expected to perform.

For immediate purposes the 'nature of the subject' means whether work in that subject calls largely for imaginative powers, as might movement and dance, or linguistic ability, as might a language, or for deductive reasoning, as might geometry.

It is worth noting in passing that the nature of economics is far from self-evident to the layman, and so many headmasters may introduce it as a school subject without any real knowledge of the subject and what it might offer – there is almost certainly a contrast between those purposes which it is expected to serve and those which it really can serve. It may appear churlish to ask school headmasters to be aware of the nature of economics; if they are graduate mathematicians or linguists they would not be expected to yield a definition of history that might please an historiographer. The point in the case of economics, however, is that most of the present generation of headteachers will have never studied economics but they will have studied at some level most of the other subjects in the school curriculum. What might be sadly said of headmasters in this respect can also be said, more mutedly, of the heads of business studies departments in many colleges and, come to that, many others responsible for fashionable curriculum change. This ambiguity in the purpose of economics teaching will be explored in a later chapter since any comment must follow from a consideration of the nature of economics.

If we hurry through an overview of the nature of economics it would be something like this. The content of economics is the allocation of scarce resources between competing ends and this problem manifests itself classically in micro-economics in the concept of opportunity cost; but the problem of resource-use is present also in macro-economics and economic growth. This is hardly to say enough but it does no great violence to the meaning of words to include a modish concern with normative decision making, or economics viewed as a system, or a traditional concern with Pareto, within such an all-embracing definition. Indeed, when we come to consider the economist's paradigm it is rather useful to define one's discipline in none too strict a fashion.

This approach hardly does say enough but for a different reason. It is quite inadequate to define a discipline by referring to the subject studied; such an approach would fail to distinguish astronomy from astrology. Clearly we must look to method as well as to content and there are plenty of prestigious precedents. Keynes: 'The theory of economics is a method rather than a doctrine, an apparatus of the mind, a technique of thinking, which helps its possessor to draw correct conclusions.'[1]

The modern treatment of the nature of economics continues this emphasis on method. An emphasis on a subject's method does not, of course, define a subject otherwise we would be unable to distinguish algebra from geometry since both are deductive in their method. When we come to define a subject we must clearly refer to both content and method.

Keynes talked of a technique of thinking. What is that technique? There are two answers and they are complements, not substitutes. The first is much more widely trumpeted than the second. Robbins

[1] J. M. Keynes, 'Introduction' to the Cambridge Economic Handbooks (Nisbet).

can help us with the first answer which is that the economist's method is deductive. 'The nature of economic analysis . . . consists of deductions from a series of postulates, the chief of which are almost universal facts of experience'[2] or again, 'The propositions of economic theory, like all scientific theory, are obviously deductions from a series of postulates. And the chief of these postulates are all assumptions involving in some way simple and indisputable facts of experience, relating to the way in which the scarcity of goods, which is the subject-matter of our science, actually shows itself in the world of reality.'[3]

Whatever else, the meaning is clear. It is a simple and indisputable fact of experience that inputs are not perfect substitutes for one another, that an extra farm worker is not the same as an extra farm field. Because they are not perfect substitutes we have the phenomenon of diminishing returns at the margin and so we can deduce something about short-run behaviour of both costs and firms. So that the origin of some of the conclusions of firm theory are to be found, at least in part, in a simple and indisputable fact of experience. Quite sophisticated theories of the firm have as part of their basis that workers are different from fields.

The deductive method is certainly widespread in economics and its pervasiveness has many implications for the teacher – not least that in this side of economics there is no room for disputatious argument. Once a firm's objective is specified as profit-maximization then it follows as a matter of logic, and not of opinion, that the price-output strategy consistent with that goal is that which equates marginal revenue and costs. It follows just as formally that a profit-maximizing monopolist will charge a price where the demand elasticity is just greater than one.

It is this very deductiveness that makes some economics tutorials so difficult. If the students really do understand there is practically nothing to do. So, at the worst, we spend tutorial time in trying to discover whether they understand – that is in examining rather than teaching. At least part of the answer to that difficulty lies in a problem-solving approach, of which more anon.

Two teaching points emerge when dealing with this deductive

[2] Lord Robbins, *Nature and Significance of Economic Science* (Macmillan, 2nd ed. 1952), p. 99.
[3] Ibid., p. 78.

part of economics. Firstly, why do some teachers always use notes? If the answer is necessarily true, if it is entailed by the assumptions, then they should be able to deduce the answer. Like teachers of mathematics we should be able to work out the answers on the board and not need reminders in front of us. Like them we need sheaves of problems and not proofs that m.r. $= P(1-\frac{1}{e})$ or whatever. If colleagues carry notes for therapeutic reasons that is one thing at this level, but any other reason is rather alarming. Second, the deductive nature of some economics means that in teaching it we should ourselves be using the deductive process self-evidently rather than, for instance, asserting.

We need to say rather more about this deductive side to economics. The views of Popper in particular need to be allowed. Robbins' original position was that the relevance of a theory could be judged by the intuitive appeal of its postulates and that it was possible to have both certainty (irrefutability) and empirical content. In practice, economists have not been in much agreement about just what is plausible but Popper's critique was more fundamental in holding, as I understand it and in summary, that a theory could only have empirical content if it had predictive powers and its predictions laid it open to refutation rather than proof. So empirical content went with refutability rather than the desirable state of having been verified. So the most that we could hope for was the tentative plausibility of not having been disproved.

We have here two apparently opposing claims. Necessarily true on the one hand and tentativeness on the other, but we are not really trying to have it both ways. We are saying that this kind of economics is a body of deductive and necessary truths, it is its relevance that is tentative. The Cobb-Douglas characteristics, for instance, are matters of logic not of opinion, while their relevance is a matter of tentative opinion.

This kind of approach, with various qualifications and emphases, such as those of Friedman, is probably reasonably common ground among economists. Unfortunately, what is also common is to overemphasize ludicrously the one kind of reasoning in the teaching of economics at the expense of the other. This overemphasis occurs in courses, and in the introductory comments on the nature of the subject in lecture courses and in many textbooks. We would all be better off if we presented ourselves as not only concerned with the necessarily true – indeed if that were so there could be no economic arguments of the current kind on inflation.

For deductive reasoning is not the only kind of good reasoning and not the only kind found in economics.

Inductive reasoning is the second part of the answer to Keynes' technique of thinking.

Inductive reasoning starts not with a premise but with real-world facts, or sets of facts, and then proceeds to an explanation. The explanation is not entailed by the facts as necessarily true for it is tentative and can have quite respectable rivals. Thus one might see an apparent relationship between the output of bacon and the price of eggs and seek to explain one by reference to the other. However 'good' the statistical techniques and results, one could soon find alternative explanations that linked the price of eggs to personal income levels or, even, the number of chickens. Quite different enquiries might all produce encouraging results and none need have a logical mistake in the sense of two and two are five.

The deductive/inductive distinction is now clear enough. The former is necessarily true, the latter is merely plausible and reasonable. And that difference should show in our teaching. The logical status of our conclusions should be quite explicit. One set of our results is deduced and the other set is reasonably inferred. These are not the same animals at all; only some of the latter are true. The differences should show in our teaching methods and the way we present our material. The Cobb-Douglas result that

$$\text{A.C.} = \frac{\text{TC}}{q} = \frac{wq_a^{\iota-1}}{b_a^{\iota}} + \frac{F}{q}$$

is not the same thing at all as Pratten and Dean cost estimations.

This brings us to an important point. We can inquire of a deductive argument: is it valid or invalid? And, given time and patience, we can yield an unambiguous yes/no answer to the question because the answers are necessarily true. We can focus on the whole problem – and the teaching problem – of intuitive reasoning by asking ourselves by what criteria we accept those propositions which are not necessary propositions. Reluctantly, we must resort to phrases like 'it gives good ground for . . .' or 'a presumption arises that . . .' The grounds of an inductive argument do not entail its conclusion; they simply support it.

Now what kind of support do we look for in inductive

economics? Clearly the answer is statistical support. And the statistical techniques to which we look are broadly those of inference and probability.

Three points: first, there seems no analytic reasoning for stressing the deductive aspect of economics against the inductive although this is exactly what most textbooks and courses do. Second, given that inductive reasoning does have a role in economics, how can we regard so-called economics courses that ignore statistical inductive techniques, as other than fraudulent, or at least distorted? Examples that leap to mind are the London External BSc(Econ.) and BA (General), most GCE A level and most HND/C courses. These courses may be valuable in some sense but no claim can be made that they give at any level a proper view of modern economics, for statistics is part of the economics. The traditional and, in my view, booby-trap distinction between theoretical and applied economics turns on this point. No such distinction is worthwhile; economics, as I shall later argue, is indivisible. And there are grave problems of teaching so-called applied economics unless the students know some statistics. Third, once one acknowledges this inductive aspect of economics then a modish problem-solving approach becomes very attractive.

I hope I have so far made it clear that the link between teaching and the nature of economics gives rise to many good questions and (some) good answers. Before I return to some of these issues I wish to develop in detail the implications for pedagogic techniques of the deductive, and then the inductive, nature of economics.

First, there is the question of language. The language in which one teaches is determined by asking not only about the nature of the subject but also to whom it is taught. In deciding how to teach we must consider not only what is being taught but also who is being taught. I think that Cohen and Cyert can help us here. 'In the deductive process, a number of different languages can be used to derive conclusions from assumptions. . . . In the past, economists have commonly used three types of language: ordinary prose, pictorial geometry and mathematics. There is now a fourth type of language which is increasingly used by economists: computer programming. There is no particular honorific ranking of theories on the basis of the language used. The scientist chooses his language primarily as a matter of convenience, both in terms of the requirements of the problem and of his facility in handling the languages.'[4]

We might rephrase to: there is no particular honorific ranking of teaching on the basis of the language used; the teacher chooses his language primarily as a matter of convenience in terms of the requirements of the problem and of the student's facility in handling the languages. In general, it may be that deductive models might be taught verbally or with geometry but I doubt that much applied economics, or more properly, inductive reasoning, can be taught without mathematical/statistical techniques. The other possibility would be to teach the conclusions as received doctrine, but since they are really only tentative and non-disproved this approach falsifies their nature and is a false method. The students do not need the conventional answers to contemporary problems. They need something with a good deal less in-built obsolescence. This would be a weakness in a too close first-year dependence on Prest.[5]

We can see something of how to choose the appropriate language and how the nature of deductive reasoning both constrains the teacher and gives him opportunities by looking at ways of teaching comparative costs.

Whatever language is chosen it is important that the deductive or inductive nature is clear.

Classroom teaching of economic theory

The problem of classroom explanation involves problems which are common to the success of all explanations. These include the interest and ability of the pupils, the success of earlier lessons and the suitability of the material for the pupils. The solution of these and similar problems is necessary to a successful explanation in economics but is not, in itself, sufficient. It is assumed in this chapter that these problems have been dealt with and consideration is given only to the problem of the explanation itself. Similarly, it is, of course, claimed that attention to the explanation is necessary but not sufficient.

[4] K. J. Cohen and R. M. Cyert, *Theory of the Firm* (Prentice-Hall, 1965), p. 20.

[5] A. R. Prest, *United Kingdom Economy – A Manual of Applied Economics* (Weidenfeld and Nicolson, 1970).

Consideration is first given to the kind of economics normally called theoretical and usually quite clearly deductive in character. We might begin with the assumption that the classroom explanation should take account of the nature of economic reasoning. There are at least three reasons for this.

First, if the classroom explanation does not correspond in some measure to the nature of an economist's explanation, then it is unfaithful to economics and the student is not receiving an economics training at all. If, for instance, he were presented with the results of economists' deductions as received doctrine it would run entirely counter to the modern view of the nature of economics as a method leading, at best, to tentative conclusions. 'Teaching' economics in this way might successfully reach various educational goals such as an examination pass but it cannot successfully achieve the goal of imparting an economics training. In the same way, a biology teacher would be unfaithful to his science if he dealt with a problem by referring to 'mother nature and her marvellous works'. Second, if a pupil does not reason for himself but is simply presented with, perhaps, the Principle of Comparative Costs as something to remember and understand it is unlikely that he will do either of these as well as if he had reasoned the principle for himself. Third, the pupils will meet greater difficulties if they are asked to reason for themselves and, provided the material is suitably chosen, they generally respond to the challenge this presents.

There is, of course, no question of the pupils doing what the economist originally did and reasoning in almost an intellectual vacuum. The pupils are learning to understand fully what is already known, not discovering what was previously unknown. But the former, among other things, can be a training for the latter. While the two things are different, it is still possible for the classroom explanation to be similar, as an experience, to the original discovery in that 'The postulates are all assumptions involving in some way simple and indisputable facts of experience' and that 'The eventual economic propositions are obviously deductions from a series of such postulates'.

The Principle of Comparative Costs might be taught in the following way. This principle is the possibility theorem that 'If each (country) specializes in the products in which it has a *comparative advantage* (greatest relative efficiency), trade will be mutually beneficial to both regions.' The phrase to note here is 'comparative advantage' which clearly implies that absolute advantage can be ignored and thus that it is beneficial for a country to import goods that it could produce more cheaply itself.

To the average sixth-former it seems preposterous that a country should deliberately import what it can make more cheaply itself, and thus run counter to the exhortations that he reads in newspapers and sees on television. The principle may be made plausible by a more familiar version; it can then be shown to be not only plausible but true and then finally proved to be true.

The pupils can be partly familiarized with an 'apparatus of the mind, a technique of thinking which helps its possessor to draw correct conclusions' by questions about making the best use of a productive factor even if the use necessitates buying something one could make more cheaply oneself. Such a question might be: 'Why do people (who have the option) work overtime and pay somebody else to paint their house, or service their car, although the money cost is greater than would have been incurred had they done the job themselves during that time?' Most students can readily provide an answer to the effect that the individual can earn more than he is charged during that time and so can finish in pocket. This is clearly a sensible use of a factor and the principle at work is readily recognizable. It is the opportunity-cost concept central to the comparative cost argument – although few texts make this clear.

It is probably worth observing to the students that it is not a proof to show that something is plausible and known to general experience. It was once 'known' that the world was flat and it certainly seemed plausible.

The Principle of Comparative Costs needs to be proved by deductive reasoning from stated assumptions. The pupils could be provided with a hypothetical example such as the following:

Production of	Good X	Good Y	
Country A	10	5	(units)
Country B	5	10	(units)
World production	15	15	

They are then told that there is no international trade between the two countries and that each engages in the production of both goods in the quantities indicated. It is then postulated, firstly, that country A uses the same input of factors to produce 10 X as it does to produce 5 Y. Thus the cost of producing 5 of Y is that 10 of X must be foregone. The reverse is true for B. Second, the very example postulates that each of the two countries is better than the other at one of the goods in the sense that production of one of the goods involves foregoing less of the other good than in the other country.

They are then told that this provides the simplest example of the gains from internatonal trade.

They are then asked for reasons why one country might be more successful than the other at producing a given good. It may be necessary to guide them on to the right lines by asking a question to which the answer is self-evident – such as why grapes are not commercially grown in England. With or without this kind of hint, they will soon suggest reasons scuh as climate, mineral resources, technical knowledge and the like, and it is probably convenient to categorize these for them under the jargon term 'factor endowments'. These matters of unequal mineral resources and so on are Robbins' 'facts of experience' and the figures given are merely an arithmetic expression of them.

The pupils are then required to draw out the implications of the figures and the postulates.

They are asked for the effect on world output if each country now concentrates on the good for which it has the favourable factor endowments. The answer is clearly:

	Good X	Good Y
Country A	20	—
Country B	—	20
World production	20	20

and they can see that the world output has increased by a third for each good. It should be emphasized that world output rises, and each country can be better off with trade than without, simply by the transfer of resources from one industry to another. There is no need to suppose, for instance, that when one country specializes in one good it will gain any of the potential benefits of specialization such as the division of labour.

There are still theoretical difficulties to come of which the most obvious is how this extra production is divided between the two countries.

The above approach is more demanding, more convincing and more faithful to the nature of economics than those accounts which say that because you are more likely to produce more per hour if you specialize, therefore international trade is beneficial. This whole assumption about specialization is redundant to the explanation which relies solely on the re-allocation of resources within both countries to yield a greater output. It is too easy, unless care is taken, for pupils to think that the principle of comparative costs depends necessarily on the division of labour.

Much greater difficulty arises for pupils in the case of trade between countries when one of the countries is better than the other at both goods. Again the teacher is unfaithful to the nature of economics, and not giving an economic education at all, if he takes refuge in unquantifiable, unverifiable generalizations about the possible benefits of the division of labour, even though in fact they may be widely applicable. The pupils must again be asked to make their own deductions from universal 'facts of experience'.

They could be given the following examples:

	Good X	Good Y
Country A	15	10
Country B	5	5
World production	20	15

This again is the situation without trade. And again country A uses the same factor input to produce either 15 of X or 10 of Y and country B uses the same input for 5 of Y or 5 of X.

Clearly country A is best at both goods but it is obviously much better at X than it is at Y compared with country B because, for the same input, it can make twice as much Y as can country B but three times as much X. It has an *absolute* advantage in both goods (and the pupils have already seen that absolute advantages are irrelevant) but it has the greater *relative* advantage at the X industry.

The pupils might now well be reminded of the man paying more for the service of his car than it would have cost him to do it himself and realize that the first case with X and Y is a very simple case with each country efficient at one good and inefficient at the other good. It is like the case of Britain importing grapes from Spain and exporting steel products. They are now facing a situation in which one country imports goods which it could make more cheaply itself and another country exports a product which it makes relatively inefficiently.

The students are asked to deduce for themselves the effect of country A concentrating its resources on the product at which it has the greatest advantage and country B concentrating on the production of the good in which it has the *least disadvantage*. The result is apparently:

	Good X	Good Y
Country A	30	—
Country B	—	10
World production	30	10

Once again, the output of each country of its own particular good has doubled merely by the transfer of resources and no allowance has been made for any extra production due to the division of labour. The pupils must now be convinced that international trade is beneficial even though the output of one of the products has diminished. They must see that 30 of X plus 10 of Y is preferable to 20 of X plus 20 of Y.

It is pointed out to them that A now has 30 of X and wants some Y and that, previously, before international trade, A obtained 1 of Y by giving up 1½ of X. The question now becomes, is it possible for A to obtain units of Y and give up less than 1½ of X for each unit. If the answer is in the affirmative, then the trade is worthwhile – *even though they are importing something they can make more cheaply themselves and even though world output of Y has decreased.*

Country B has all the Y and requires some X. Previously B got X by giving up 1 unit of Y for every unit of X. The situation for B is that trade is beneficial for both of them if it takes place so that between 1½ and 1 of X are traded for each unit of Y. There is insufficient information to say where the rate of exchange between the goods will be between these two limits. That is a separate question for yet more deductive reasoning.

The pupils should now realize that the case for international trade depends on changing the *ratios* at which goods must be foregone if some are to be obtained at the expense of the other. The possibility of greater *amounts* due to specialization can then be introduced as a possible (and likely) extra advantage of international trade and it can be made clear that international trade is beneficial even without it.

Similar opportunities frequently offer themselves for the use of this teaching technique. It is, for instance, preferable for the pupils to be presented with an arithmetic example of the costs and revenues that a firm might meet at different levels of output and asked to identify the point of maximum profits, and to note its characteristics, rather than that they should be informed that profits are maximized when marginal revenue equals marginal costs.[6] They would again be proceeding from their own experience, in this case of manipulating figures, to a principle of wide applicability.

The case for presenting the pupils with a situation in which they have to deduce for themselves can be briefly summarized. It is more likely that they will remember the economic theory, realize its significance, have confidence in it and be able to make use of it. There is, of course, no question of claiming that such a technique is, in itself, sufficient to guarantee effective learning. The complete solution lies in matters outside this chapter, such as the choice of material.

This whole attitude to a successful explanation lies in a distinction between knowledge and understanding. The relevant difference between the two can be shown by the following example. A student could be presented with the information that Napoleon lost the battle of Waterloo, or that profits are maximized where marginal costs and revenue are equated, and he might be persuaded to remember the information and to believe it. But he has had no training as a historian, or as an economist, unless he also has some understanding of the explanation in the sense of knowing why it was Wellington who won and not Napoleon, and why profits are maximized not where total revenue is highest but where marginal costs and revenue are equated. It seems very reasonable to the average sixth-former, for instance, that a firm should want to increase its total revenue and they are unlikely to see that this can be a mistaken policy if they have not deduced for themselves the optimal output and the reciprocal relationships between output and the various kinds of costs and revenues

[6] See Chapter 3 for a more detailed account of the advantages and disadvantages of this and other methods of dealing with this problem.

In turning now to inductive reasoning I wish to play down any distinction between theoretical and applied economics. As Marion Bowley put it to her students, 'The only difference is that theory is about A and B and applied is about apples and pears.' Quite clearly, this is the correct emphasis. The only worthwhile applied economics is that which is informed by theory. In contrast, it is better to re-emphasize the knowledge-understanding trade-off. As Bentham put it: 'When we have words in our ears, we think we have ideas in our heads.' It is a technique of thinking we are after and not contemporary facts: it is the *idea* of a Customs Union (trade diversion/creation etc.) which marks us out from other disciplines and not the details of any particular one.

In looking at economic inductive reasoning we can find at least four separate forms of reasoning. Probably most applied problems call on more than one form of reasoning rather than fit neatly into a single pigeon-hole. We seem to use historical, colligational, evaluatory and quantitative reasoning. That is probably the rising order of importance.

Quite obviously we do resort to historical introduction if we are discussing SDRs, the location of the car industry in Luton or the role of the Bank of England. I propose to say nothing more for the moment about the problems of history teaching. In describing some explanations as 'colligational' in nature, it may be that I am bending the meaning of the word. What I, at least, mean is that some explanations succeed by referring to a number of factors, all of which in themselves are necessary, none of which are in themselves sufficient, and all of which together may be sufficient. Clearly the availability of suitable land at Luton is necessary but not sufficient in explaining the location of the car industry.

What seems to me important in all this is that the logical status of the explanation should be very clear because of the way it has been taught. It *must* be self-evident that each location is unique in itself and not an example of some general 'law' that all available land is populated with car factories. It *is* common for overseas GCE candidates to describe their own central bank as though it were the Bank of England uprooted and placed in another country and city thus implying some general 'law' about central banks. Many essays, examination answers and projects that touch on such matters lead to this kind of absurdity and it is simply because the teacher did not make the sufficient/necessary distinction. There can be no more abusive comment on the average polytechnic economics teacher than the average HND project.

The evaluatory part of applied economics is normally what is now fashionably called Applied Welfare Economics.

Two clear advantages of teaching this kind of applied economics are that, firstly, it emphasizes the real need, as opposed to fashion, for empirical testing in economics. Second, this kind of teaching forces the student up against the scientific nature of genuine economics as against the ascientific nature of public discussion about, say, the Third London Airport. This is an attractive menu but there is an immediate difficulty and consequent syllabus implication. Nothing worthwhile can be done along these lines until the student has some reasonably effective grip on optimizing conditions and the Second Best problem. Although it is a worthy desire to make economics useful (and therefore attractive?) we might as well recognize that it is a long haul. Nor should we be surprised – would you like a first-year medical student to take out your appendix?

It is doubtless possible to overplay this point and some exceptions can be readily produced. What does need emphasizing, however, is that one- and two-year courses of subsidiary economics cannot really offer these kinds of advantages and must be justified by rather different criteria. And we may certainly be sceptical of those BA (General), HND/C, GCE courses that ask policy questions and exclude welfare economics from the syllabus. In a sense the question is whether or not economics is worth doing for a few hours for a year or two. We ought not simply to assume that the answer is 'yes' but to think carefully about the syllabus implications and objectives of such a course.

Applied welfare economics is well worth doing but we will never do it well unless we acknowledge explicitly the logical standing of the kind of explanation being offered, and also its limited applicability since most of these problems also pose normative non-economic questions.

Much the same can be said of the more explicitly quantitative kind of inductive economics. Anybody who has reluctantly allowed a DMS/HND/C student to attempt something like a cost-benefit analysis, within a public sector industry employing him, knows how little can be done until a great deal of economics has been learnt, *although the student may be able to write quite good essays about CBA*. Similar, though more muted, comments are in order in the case of linear programming.

It is helpful in quantitative economics to eliminate barriers between economics as conventionally defined and other subjects normally taught separately such as statistics and OR. The historical distinctions between these subjects are quite arbitrary and, more to the point, damaging. For ordinary, timetabling purposes, there have to be some separations, but we sell our student short by allowing these to structure the student's perceptions of the nature of economics. I am not here advocating that we embrace quantitative techniques because it is fashionable to do so, for it was the students of my generation who were sold short by being presented with economics as though it started, and indeed finished, within the covers of Stonier and Hague.[7] Economics is indivisible from these techniques and it always has been, but this has not always been made clear in the way the subject has been taught.

Statistical or results must not be presented as received doctrine. The students must, as soon as possible, meet significance tests, degrees of freedom, etc., in the ordinary course of economics. This will also have the added benefit that they will regard the facts of applied economics as 'facts'. And the status of what is being claimed will be all the clearer.

It is fashionable, and properly so, to indulge in econometric techniques. What is less emphasized, but just as important, is a respect for the sources and tentativeness of the facts. There is no analytic reason to emphasize one against the other. There is every reason to include both within contemporary economics for otherwise we cannot properly cope with inductive reasoning in seeking explanations of real-world problems.

Before I pass on to problems of presentation and communication I should like to underline some of the advantages to the teacher of making the logical status of our explanations quite explicit whether we are dealing with the deductive or inductive.

---

[7] As I was taught by both these authors I should say that neither ever intended their book to be treated in this manner. The courses now offered at Professor Hague's Manchester Business School do not recognize arbitrary distinctions between economics and other subjects.

A clear advantage is that in presenting economics in this way the theoretical basis should be quite explicit. And one of the great shortcomings of some so-called applied economics has been this separation from a theoretical discipline. It really is remarkable at what length colleagues can write about monopoly policy as though removing any one monopoly unambiguously improved welfare. Second, by harping on the nature of what we are doing we would separate out the quantifiable from the non-quantifiable and could not help but emphasize the differences between these two kinds of assertions.

We can see the profit in relating teaching methods to the nature of the subject by looking briefly at the sad history of the teaching of cost curves. For many years they were persistently U-shaped in textbooks and persistently L-shaped in empirical tests. Textbooks tended to suppress the latter as inconvenient for the former. We would all have been a great deal better off if textbooks had presented the U-shapeness as necessarily true on certain specifications and the L-, and any other, shapeness as the results of inductive reasoning on quite different specifications. The two 'conclusions' could have then appeared side by side instead of one getting the Stalin treatment as ideologically inconvenient. We only thought there was a difficulty because we did not fully understand the differing natures of the two things that we were doing, that is that $\frac{dc}{dq}/v = 0$ is not the same as $\frac{dc}{dv}/q = 0$! A change in rate of output is different from a change in volume of output.

In passing, it might be noted that in seeking a pattern, or gestalt, economics teachers, if not economists, face a booby-trap in that too much can be explained if the pattern is convincing. Sweezy's Kinked Demand curve model is not alone in being a particular case mistaken for a general case, and then swept into textbooks because it was understandable and neat. Its strength was that it solved a problem for teachers on introductory courses and not that it was really a general case to correspond to the monopoly and competition general cases.

A further point remains to be considered in this chapter. Some economists admit not only of theoretical and applied economics but also of 'descriptive economics'. This usually seems to mean topics such as the geographical distribution of the population or the functions of joint-stock banks.

It is a misuse of the term to call such factual accounts 'economics'. They would be better categorized as 'commerce'. Once an explanation of the facts is offered there seems to be no significant difference from applied economics. Topics like the joint-stock banks are also studied by lawyers, sociologists and occupational psychologists and most economists' problems are shared with other disciplines. The economic aspects are identified and explained by regarding the topic through a special pair of spectacles, as it were, and they will not be provided by a solely factual 'descriptive economics' lesson.

It is sometimes put that this is a too heavy-handed dismissal of descriptive economics because one can hardly explain something one cannot describe. It might well be answered that to explain behaviour is to specify it and it might be recalled that physicists could explain the behaviour of atomic neutrons and positrons long before they could be described in this sense. All that need be said for the moment is that to describe only is hardly the usual specification of the economist's role and that it is difficult to see the educational benefit of only describing – whatever role it is.

An earlier possible misapprehension is worth re-emphasizing. In discussing empirical testing we have referred to the 'tentative conclusions' of economics. Elsewhere we have talked of 'logically necessary' conclusions. This is not, in fact, having it both ways. It is not the internal consistency that is tentative of the profit-maximization model but whether it is the appropriate model at all to 'explain' a firm's behaviour. Empirical results are always tentative, as Popper has emphasized, and so is whether we have asked the right questions (which is the equivalent of making the right postulates), but not the internal consistency of the deduced answers to those questions we have in fact asked.

The attitude of this chapter can now be summarized by saying that if a classroom explanation is to be a valid training in economics and is to be a correct explanation, then it must take account of the kind of reasoning used in economics. Several kinds of explanations are used in different aspects of economics so consequently there is no single technique that can be applied to every lesson and, because some problems do not fit neatly into any of the conventional categories of economics, there will necessarily be some lessons where several explanatory methods must be used together.

The next chapter takes a further look at the teaching of theoretical economics and also at the implications for the classroom of the various forms of explanation used in applied economics.

No modern discussion of the nature of economics can fail to make at least some passing mention of the notion of an economics paradigm. This focuses neither on the method nor the content of a discipline and is a slippery term to define and to make manifest in economics. A paradigm specifies the type of relationship to be investigated by a recognized discipline and also the methods and abstractions to be regarded as legitimate. It thus both defines the problems for a science and the methods of solving them. Thus, the economist would not normally regard the structure of a nationalized industry as part of his problem but he would so regard its pricing and investment policies. It may be that at this moment economics does not have a closely specified paradigm like those apparently available in natural sciences. It may also not be clear just how we recognize phenomena that fall within our own paradigm, but we do all recognize without fail that much of what is published in *The Economist* is not economics. You know it when you see it, or at least you know most of it when you see it, and very little is open to dispute as a legitimate problem for the profession.

Another feature of a paradigm is that it may have restrictive effects on both research and teaching in a discipline. For the paradigm structures the whole intellectual approach to a problem. In Kuhn's phrase, a profession makes 'a strenuous and devoted effort to force nature into the conceptual boxes supplied by professional education'. Thus in economics, both courses and textbooks taught U-shaped cost-curves and their empirical L shape was either ignored or left in footnotes. Once Alchian and Hirschliefer had shown that, by re-specifying the kind of cost change under discussion, it was possible to have both U and L shapes in the theory, then L-shapeness could appear in quite elementary textbooks. It was wonderful. We could have it both ways. The theoreticians and the real world were compatible. To repeat, the paradigm both defines the problems and the methods of solving them. It gives us intellectual tunnel vision.

It might be noted that all this exactly specifies the difficulties with modish inter-disciplinary courses. If a course integrates, say, economics and sociology then there is an absence of criteria with which to judge the content or the level. The economics paradigm is irrelevant and so is the behavioural scientist's. There is no paradigm save that of high fashion and goodwill. This, of course, specifies the difficulties and nothing more.

It is the aspect of defining legitimate areas of work that has teaching implications for us. I see very clearly, as Gertrude Stein would say, that the profession was wrong to keep l.p. techniques at arm's length for so long in college courses and that some of what has tended to appear within the province of accountants and OR specialists is ours as much as theirs but, despite some prestigious advocacy, I am rather doubtful that there is much profit in a link with the behaviourial sciences.

Attempts have been made to identify the 'core' of economics; Lumsden and Attiyeh have claimed that economics is concerned with objectives, the formulation of theories and the testing of hypotheses and that all proper economics courses must treat exgenous and endogenous variables, interdependence and the problems of aggregation and marginal analysis. They offer as fundamental concepts: scarcity and choice, economic efficiency, income distribution and aggregate output and income.[8] This kind of menu approach misses the point of a paradigm and, perhaps, was not designed to that end.

Economics is concerned with allocation and thus with interdependence but we are far better off thinking of economics as a system and as being about decision making. From time to time we alter what is the appropriate part of the system to study, and, indeed, our own view of the system. The view that the Keynesian model is a special case of the neo-classical model is an example, as is the view that the Keynesian model is fundamentally different. Economics is a system and the main concept seems to be that of equilibrium: its specification and the dynamic adjustments between equilibria. A Kuhnian view of science and its developments leads us also to feel that problem-solving is central to economics – both as an objective and as a teaching-technique. An entire chapter is later devoted to this.

[8] K. G. Lumsden and R. E. Attiyeh, 'The Core of Basic Economics', *Economics*, Vol. 9, pt 1 (No. 37) Summer 1971, pp. 33–40.

Perhaps, in summarizing, I might pre-empt some of the opposing arguments.

I am advancing a necessary but insufficient theme. Of course, a comprehensive account of the teaching of economics would deal with other problems that this approach ignores, and bring other criteria to those problems which we have touched upon, but it seems clear that no proper understanding either of the role of economics or of teaching methods is possible without some attention to the nature of the subject.

To provide a rationale for a redefinition of economics is simply to intellectualize what is already occurring. And the same applies in encouraging mathematics as an appropriate language. What is less remarked on is that when we teach a non-mathematized economics, or ignore inductive procedures, simply asserting 'facts', or when we pass by OR techniques, then we are teaching not only a little economics but are also distorting its nature. If a student only studies nineteenth-century economic history then he knows only a little economic history but he may well have been exposed to quite genuine historical explanations. Our difficulty is that when we teach a little economics we also present at least slightly bogus economic explanations.

This is not an empire-building plea that says all or nothing. It may well be that the benefits of teaching a little economics exceed the costs but we should be quite explicit that one of the costs is a view of economics that is out of focus.

*

CHAPTER THREE   Classroom Techniques

This chapter is concerned with the techniques of the economics teacher in the classroom. The emphasis thus shifts from the general need to take account of the nature of economic analysis to the practical problems of teaching. The teacher's role is to take either information or expertise and modify it in such a way that the student can most easily master it. However, great care must be taken with the modification lest it becomes a distortion.

The distinction between modification and distortion is a most critical one; all distortions are modifications but there is no need for modifications to distort their subject. The teacher must bear the difference in mind as he selects material for his lesson and the method to be adopted in teaching it. The method of teaching must be chosen from a wide range of possibilities. The teacher can resort to an oral account during which the students take their own notes, to informal group discussions, to visual aids or to some combinations of these and many other alternatives. Attention will first be paid to the arrangement of the material which it is hoped the student will absorb and then to the various methods of communicating it.

The presentation of material

This involves two separate but overlapping problems: the data must not be presented in a haphazard manner but in an intelligible manner so that it may easily be remembered, but also this intelligible pattern must accord with the nature of the subject.

It is easy to modify almost any material so that it can be recollected easily, but it is more difficult to make sure that at the same time a disciplined academic training is given. There seem to be three main ways of presenting information so that it can easily be remembered.

In the first place, use can be made of some memory trick, thus the trigonometrical rule that the ratio of the base to the hypotenuse equals the cosine can be remembered by recalling that BHC are the initials of the mathematics master. Clearly, such a teaching device has no explanatory powers whatsoever and is in no sense a mathematical training. This is not to say that it is not an effective memory trick and that the student could not apply the rule successfully; it does say that the student can have gained no mathematical appreciation. Second, material can be more easily remembered if it is arranged in a pattern that makes some use of the subject being taught, without in fact being an academic training, although it may appear to the student that it is indeed academic analysis. For example, the location of the hat industry in Luton might be explained by referring to the local supplies of straw in the days of straw hats but it would hardly be a training in economics. Third, material can be arranged in an intelligible pattern and at the same time the pattern can acknowledge the nature of the subject, so that the very arrangement of the material is itself a training in economics.

A frivolous, but convenient, example of how a pattern may be imposed on material so that it appears analytic, when in fact it distorts the material, is afforded by the habit of analysing modern football strategies in numerical terms. Thus England's World Cup victory was 'explained' by reference to the 4–3–3 formation. Two observations seem to be in order. First, it needs to be emphasized that this is not a sufficient explanation. If all sixteen teams adapted this formation, fifteen would have to lose. Second, it is not really a helpful way of thinking about that team since *The Times* printed the team as Banks, Cohen, Charlton J., Stiles, Wilson, Moore, Charlton R., Ball, Hurst, Hunt, Peters, while the *Guardian* printed it as Banks, Cohen, Charlton J., Moore, Wilson, Stiles, Charlton R., Peters, Ball, Hurst, Hunt. In other words, although the 4–3–3 way of organizing the resources was much mentioned it is by no means apparent how the resources (the players) fit into this formation, and so it was an explanatory arrangement that appeared more helpful than it really was.

An example of the problems of arranging economic material is

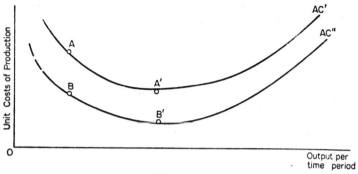

Figure I

afforded by the problems in teaching 'economies of scale'; they are illustrated in figure I.

The cost curves show how economists expect average costs of production would change as the scale of output is increased – that it is thought that the resources needed for each unit produced would at first fall but eventually rise. A.C.' represents the effect on costs of increasing production while the firm operates with some of its productive resources fixed, perhaps the amount and kind of machinery used, while A.C." shows the effect on costs of operating with other factors fixed. Thus each cost curve represents a different method of production.

It is immediately apparent that costs can fall in three separate ways for quite different reasons and that these must be carefully separated for the pupil. Costs might fall in the way represented by A–B and this means that a new method of production is being used. The same output is now produced for less input and the economist explains this by reference to the concept of 'efficiency'. This is quite separate from a cost change such as A – A' which also involves less input per unit of output but by changing output rather than method. The economist's explanation depends largely on the concept of 'economies of scale'. A third possibility is shown by A – B' in which the firm alters both the method and the scale of output. The period of time in which the firm cannot alter its method is the *short-run* and the *long-run* is the period in which it can. Thus it can move A – A' in the short-run but A – B/B' only in the long-run.

The student can only be taught economies of scale successfully if the material is arranged so that he realizes that some decreases in costs are attributable to more efficient production and some to greater production. Those in the second category are properly termed economies of scale and they are divided into those attainable in the short-run and those attainable in the long-run. The pupil will need explanations of why A – A', A – B and A – B' change costs but it is preferable for the pattern of these explanations to be arranged in the above way.

If economies of scale are simply listed and explained as being attributable to: 'indivisibilities', 'increased dimensions', 'specialization', 'massed resources', 'superior organization', and the 'learning effect'[1] then each explanation might well be competent but the material would not have been arranged in the way most easily remembered or in the way most effective as a training in economics. What is more, the actual arrangement of the material might be mistaken by the student for something of serious analytic significance.

Having illustrated by example the importance of arranging correct material in a particular way, the next thing is to show how material can be arranged in theoretical economics and in the various kinds of applied economics.

One of the problems of the teaching of theoretical economics is to explain to the student why firms maximize their profits when marginal revenue equals marginal cost. The material necessary for the concept to be remembered and understood can be arranged in a number of ways. The guiding principles seem to be that the material should be presented in such a way that the deduction is clear and rigorous and within the intellectual grasp of the student. As mentioned earlier, attention must be paid to *who* is being taught as well as to *what* is being taught. From the range of possible teaching arrangements within the pupil's grasp, the one should be chosen which teaches him most with the least risk of ambiguity. In other words, the teacher's modification of his material must take account of the demands of the pupil and the subject; sometimes these are irreconcilable and so a presumption arises that economics is unsuitable for those pupils.

Firstly, profit maximization might be taught using differential

[1] C. Pratten and R. M. Dean, *The Economies of Large Scale Production in British Industry* (Cambridge University Press, 1965), pp. 18–19.

calculus thus: $R = P.Q - C$ when R represents profits, P represents price, Q represents output and C represents costs. Profits are maximized when they are differentiated with respect to output, viz:

$$\frac{dR}{dQ} = \frac{dPQ}{dQ} - \frac{dCQ}{dQ} = O \text{ or } \frac{d(PQ)}{dQ} = \frac{dC}{dQ}$$

But to say that profits are maximized when $\frac{d(PQ)}{dQ} = \frac{dC}{dQ}$ is to say that they are maximized when marginal revenue and cost are equated, since $\frac{d(PQ)}{dQ}$ is merely an expression for marginal revenue and $\frac{dC}{dQ}$ is simply an expression for marginal cost.

Clearly such a technique could only be used if the students already had sufficient expertise in the relevant kind of mathematics. This is a necessary condition for such a lesson and such a teaching method would be neat and economical for those able to benefit from it. It would be wholly unsuitable for non-mathematical students. The above explanation is limited in that it fails to draw attention to the fact that the equality of marginal revenue and marginal costs is merely a necessary condition and not a sufficient one. However, students able to cope with the above would also appreciate that they had merely been shown the first-order condition and that the second-order condition was that $\frac{d^2(pQ)}{dQ^2}$ should be negative, that is the firm should already have been making profits when marginal revenue became equal to marginal cost.

A second teaching method, and again one really suitable only to the mathematically adept student, relies on a diagram with tangents to total revenue and total cost curves such as figure 2. Profits are maximized where the interval between total revenue and total costs is the greatest as at the output Q^I. The student can see by observation that at such a point the tangents to the curves are parallel whereas at Q^{II} they are diverging, showing that the interval between total revenue and total costs can be increased by expanding output while the reverse is true of Q^{III} where they converge and profits can be increased by contracting output. However, only the mathematically

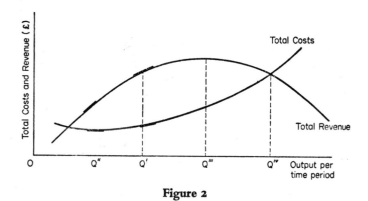

Figure 2

trained will realize that the tangents to total revenue and total costs are exactly the same concepts as marginal cost and marginal revenue.

This way of arranging exactly the same evidence is clearly only suitable for a limited range of students but it has advantages over the first method in that it shows concisely that the maximization of profits (Q'), profitable output (Q''''), and profitable revenue (Q'''), are not necessarily the same thing.[2] It is important to emphasize the difference between these various concepts; students who have simply been told that profits are maximized where marginal revenue equals marginal costs, or have been shown a proof that uses a poor teaching technique, are soon talking of maximizing revenue instead of profits. The points can be made clearly enough from figure 2. Thus, this second method demonstrates that profits are maximized when marginal revenue equals marginal cost and it draws attention to a number of related and significant points, but its great drawback is that only those students with some appreciation of mathematics will grasp the full concept of tangency as an expression of the rate of change of costs or revenue, that is of marginal costs or revenue.

A third method avoids mathematical difficulties by producing simple arithmetic tables of price, output, total revenue and costs, marginal revenue and costs and profit. This method is easily compre-

[2] This could also be demonstrated by using the sort of expression found of the first teaching method given but it would need a rather longer proof than in the second method. However, it would not be a difficult proof.

hended although it is somewhat cumbersome but its chief difficulty is that it can raise a problem the answer to which is only really significant to those who are mathematically adroit. The method begins by defining marginal revenue, marginal costs and the other concepts and then presents the student with some table such as the following.

Output	Price	Total revenue	Marginal revenue	Total cost	Marginal cost	Profits
0	0	0	–	1	–	– 1
1	10	10	10	10	9	0
2	9	18	8	16	6	2
3	8	24	6	20	4	4
4	7	28	4	24	4	4
5	6	30	2	28	4	2
6	5	30	0	32	4	– 2
7	4	28	– 2	37	5.	– 9
8	3	24	– 4	43	6	–19
9	2	18	– 6	50	7	–32
10	1	10	– 8	60	10	–50

The difficulty with this and similar tables is that profits are sometimes maximized at two different levels of output, three units and four units in this case, and at only one of them are marginal costs and revenue equal. Such a table thus produces a new problem and so makes a poor teaching method; not only does it fail to convince the student that profits are maximized where marginal revenue equals marginal costs but the explanation of the anomaly – that the figures represent a discontinuous function in which the independent variable makes discrete changes – can only be appreciated by students with some mathematical training. It is thus an effective teaching technique in that it shields the student from the mathematical difficulties of calculus and tangents but it raises further mathematical problems!

A fourth teaching method makes use of some such diagram as figure 3. The students are taught that marginal costs can be falling, constant or rising. The diagram shows the conventional equilibrium position with falling marginal revenue and rising marginal costs and the syllabus should later take care of the other possibilities. The pupils are shown the output Q where marginal revenue and costs are equated and invited to realize the consequence of moving to other output. If output is decreased by one unit to Q′ this must change the level of profits (the diagram does not give any numerical value to profits). The new level must differ from the old by the difference between the changes in revenue and costs. Clearly, a greater amount has been lost in revenue than in costs, that is R′Q′ is a greater amount than C′Q′. It should be clear that when marginal revenue exceeds marginal costs profits can always be increased by expanding output as this will add more to revenue than to costs, so all outputs where marginal revenue is greater than costs must be sub-maximum from a profit point of view. A comparable argument can be conducted in terms of a production increase from Q to Q″. This must add more, R″ Q″ to costs than to revenue which only increases by C″ Q″. So any output where marginal costs exceeds marginal revenue must also be a sub-optimal output in that a reduction in output always takes more from costs than it does from revenue. It should thus be clear that if profits are sub-maximum

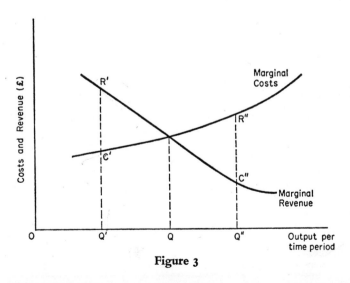

Figure 3

whenever marginal revenue is unequal to marginal costs, then profits can only be maximized when marginal revenue does equal marginal costs. Such a lesson can easily be understood provided the students are confident about the precise meaning of marginal cost and revenue. They must be quite clear that marginal revenue is the effect on total revenue of an output change and marginal costs the effect on total costs of an output change.

The difficulty with this method is that it does not draw attention to the important distinction between the idea that equality of marginal revenue and costs is a necessary characteristic and the idea that it is a sufficient condition for profit maximization. The latter notion is fallacious and the student is unlikely to raise the problem of this distinction unless it arises in the course of the explanation.

The fifth possible teaching method accommodates this difficulty. The students are shown a diagram, like figure 4, and the circumstances explained in which prices do not alter with output and why this means that price equals marginal revenue and that marginal revenue is constant at all outputs. They are also taught that average cost curves are roughly U-shaped and that marginal cost curves are also this shape and intersect the average cost curve at the nadir of the average cost curve. An explanation then follows like that in the fourth method but it is apparent now to the pupil that there are two points at which marginal revenue equals marginal cost. This is most

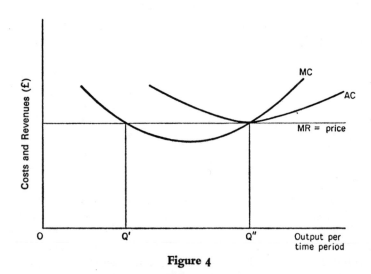

Figure 4

easily shown in the constant price case as in figure 4. It also holds for the falling price case as in figure 3. It is apparent that the output OQ' is a profit minimizing output and OQ" is a profit maximizing output. This illustrates to the student that the equality of marginal revenue and cost is only a necessary condition. It is a first-order condition, and a further condition is that the output preceding the marginal equality should have been profitable. This latter point is the second-order condition.

This last method of arranging material to teach the profit maximizing condition seems preferable for most students. It makes no unreasonable demands on his mathematical ability and it makes it clear that the equality of marginal revenue and costs is only a necessary condition. This point could quite easily be accommodated in the first teaching method for the students familiar with calculus. Nevertheless, for most sixth-form students the fifth method seems to be the technique that teaches most with the least risk of confusion.

This survey of different ways of arranging material to teach a particular point throws into relief two quite important factors. First, great attention must be paid to the order in which subjects are taught within the syllabus, so that in the above instance the pupils are already aware of the circumstances in which the firm's price equals marginal revenue before they are given the fifth version of the lessons on the profit maximizing output. Second, the teacher of economic science must arrange his material and choose a 'language' in which to express it bearing in mind the nature of the problem and the facility of his students in handling that language.

In some instances the nature of the problem may leave no real choice about the language. Where there is a choice then the teacher must choose the method of posing the problem that best accommodates the need to modify the material so that the student can grasp its significance without distorting the subject. Any account of profit maximization that implied that equating marginal revenue and costs was a sufficient condition would distort the subject, mislead the student and deceive him about the complexity of the problem. The language chosen clearly depends partly on the student's grasp of mathematics and we must realize that decisions about teaching methods cannot be taken independently of the rest of the curriculum.

The problems of sequence in the economics teaching programme is one that has proved vexatious and manifold. Macro before micro?

Supply before production? Or vice-versa? And so on. Any slight acquaintance with how economists work tells us that there is no 'correct' answer and indicates the main teaching points. The economist 'explains' product prices by holding factor prices constant and then uses the *ceteris paribus* technique to analyse factor prices. And, of course, no real comprehension of one is possible without some knowledge of the other. Similar examples abound throughout economics. Although the syllabus is divided into parts no single part can be understood without reference to the whole system and it is of no real consequence in what order the topics are presented. It is rather like the newcomer to London who, by using the Underground map, arrives at Tottenham Court Road and learns the surrounding road pattern and then learns the one around Oxford Circus and, finally, learns that the two patterns interlink into a system. It really would not matter if he had started off at Oxford Circus.

It is as well to make all this clear to the student at the beginning, so that he does not expect one topic to make complete operational sense in a kind of intellectual vacuum, and constantly to refer back and forward so that the context of the particular model is clear – which means also that its limitations will be clear.

Attention must now be given to the problem of presenting material in applied economics. Descriptive applied economics will be ignored on the ground that it is not a valid form of academic economics; historical, colligational, quantitative and evaluatory applied problems will be dealt with briefly in turn.

Those topics in applied economics which demand an historical treatment must be taught like any other historical topic in a manner that acknowledges the largely colligational nature of historical explanation. The teacher must also reverse the historian's process by leading the pupils from the pattern to the facts instead of looking at the facts first and then seeing the pattern that they reveal.[3]

There seems no further important problem in arranging the material in teaching colligational applied economics. The problem of the student mistaking a necessary condition for a sufficient condition is less likely to occur if the relevant factors are presented together at the start of the lesson so that he can grasp the general

[3] For further details see W. H. Burston, *Principles of History Teaching* (Methuen, 1963), Chapter 4, pp. 86–7.

form of the explanation before meeting a detailed analysis of some special point. Here too, the economics teacher is proceeding in the reverse order from that of the research economist. Thus there is less likelihood of a misunderstanding if the student is briefly presented with a list of all points relevant to economic growth before hearing the details of, say, labour productivity, provided it is clear that the list offers no explanations in itself and that its purpose is to give perspective. On the other hand, there is a greater likelihood of his failing to appreciate the whole pattern of economic growth if he receives successive lessons on productivity, technology, factor input-ratios and so on, without any attempt to interrelate these topics. In the author's experience students are only too eager to find 'explanations' of these problems that refer to only one factor. This emphasizes the need to state clearly that a given point is relevant and necessary but not sufficient to the explanation.

The student needs a glimpse of the whole subject before he starts so that he sees the relative importance of the different points as they occur, and probably some summary at the close of the lesson or of a series of lessons so that he can appreciate the dovetailing of the various points.

The arrangement of material in those applied economics lessons concerned with evaluations of institutions or policies must bear in mind three points. Advantages which are capable of empirical testing must be distinguished, for that reason, from those that have an unverifiable basis; the sense must be given of a 'balance' of advantages and disadvantages in an unresolved problem; and lastly, the material should, where possible, flow from a theoretical basis. This is partly to illustrate the significance of economic theory, ensuring that it is not something separate in the student's mind that he feels is only used to answer theoretical questions, and partly because it is an essential aspect of applied analysis that its theoretical basis should be explicit.

Thus currency devaluation is taught in a manner faithful to the nature of economics if it appears in a lesson as a possible technique for the government to adopt and the student sees devaluation as a policy, giving particular results to be compared with other policies and other results, rather than taking the popular view that it is a possible policy only if all else fails. The student would be made aware of the advantages and disadvantages of such a policy and

which of these have an economic content and which are wholly
political in nature. He would also be made to use his theoretical
knowledge to deduce that devaluation is only beneficial to the
Balance of Payments if the sum of the elasticities of demand for
exports and imports is greater than the one.

The material for a lesson in quantitative economics is most easily
arranged by focusing on the problem and expressing it in precise
economic terms emphasizing those variables which are to be meas-
ured, and discussing their significance, and then giving the students
the results of any measurements that have been made.

A suitable example for school courses is provided by the Board of
Trade policy of concentration in the Second World War. This was
the practice in those industries which were restricting production
by closing down some factories while others were run at full
capacity rather than the alternative policy of running all factories
at half capacity. This was argued on economic grounds as
follows.

Cost curves are thought to be U-shaped as in figure 5. If the
economy has two separate factories with identical cost curves like
those in the diagram and between them they produce an output of
twice OM and then, due to the war, output must be reduced to
OM, it is argued by some that it is more economical to close one
factory and produce OM in the other rather than to produce
OM' in both. (Assume OM' = $\frac{1}{2}$ OM.) This concentration policy

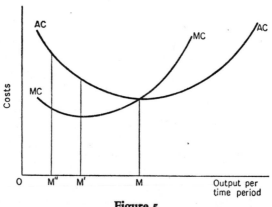

Figure 5

depends on average costs at OM being less than at OM'. This is a persuasive argument but the economist would feel that it does not ask the right question and that if the right question is asked the concentration policy will not always lead to less input per unit of output.

The significant point is that the two factories are already built and so some costs have already been incurred whether or not there is production within the factory. These costs are now inescapable and they are included in the total costs from which the average cost curves shown in the diagram are calculated. If the problem is to produce OM, given that the two factories are already built, with the least use of resources, then the whole solution turns on *minimizing the escapable* extra cost of producing OM. This is the real opportunity–cost. Thus, the significant question concentrates on marginal cost instead of average cost. It is immediately apparent from the diagram that marginal cost is less at OM' output than it is at OM and so twice OM' must be less than OM with regard to marginal costs. This means that the most efficient policy is to produce in both factories at half capacity rather than to concentrate production at one factory. This is a significant lesson for students illustrating a way of thinking that is characteristic of economists.

However, the lesson on quantitative economics must then proceed to point out the significance of starting from a position such as OM at which marginal costs were rising. If the original position is OM' and the choice is between OM' in one factory or OM" in two factories (OM" = $\frac{1}{2}$ OM') then the concentration policy is well advised since now output involves falling marginal cost per unit instead of rising marginal costs.

The teacher must arrange his material so that the student focuses on the significant aspects of the quantitative problems which, in this case, are twofold; first, the importance of marginal rather than average costs and, second, the performance of marginal costs at the original level of output, that is whether they were rising, constant or falling. This particular case makes a good problem for tutorial work intended to emphasize the operational problem-solving nature of economics.

It is difficult to say much more in general about this kind of applied economics. Different levels of economics, with and without statistics, clearly call for different emphases. What is common to all is the need to realize the significance of what has been done by identifying the nature of what has been done. A discussion, at any level, of the inductive 'evidence' on inflation would benefit from such an approach.

It is worth restating that it is not intended to imply that all problems in applied economics fall neatly into the categories of historical and 'environmental' problems and the evaluation of the institutions and policies so explained or into the category of quantitative economics. Many topics in applied economics will draw on several kinds of explanation and perhaps, also, evaluation and quantification. A study of the United Kingdom Discount Market, for instance, might well call on the techniques of the historian to explain the sources of its present structure and then might need to place the market within the whole economic environment. This might be followed by an evaluation of the Discount Market in the sense of whether its role might be performed in some other way with less use of resources, and then finally by a quantification of the costs and benefits such as, for instance, its foreign exchange earnings.

In the course of these different sorts of explanation, economists will normally have recourse to explanations of a general character such as the shape of cost curves, the identification of escapable costs or the nature of input–output ratios because (like all social scientists) they classify events into groups by noting their common characteristics and then seeking explanations of that class of event in the form of a theory of, say, cost changes.

These theories are then applied to particular events with any relevant qualifications. The economist's terminology for this is to talk of theories and then 'models' within this theory which deal with particular manifestations of the general problem being studied. The teacher's problem is to arrange the material of the lesson in such a way that the student can most effectively appreciate whatever solution the economist has to offer.

The communication of the material

It is a well-known general principle that oral exposition is a poor method of communication in that the student plays a passive role. This gives rise to two separate problems in economics: first, the efficiency of alternative techniques is also severely circumscribed and, second, there are special difficulties in teaching economics when oral methods are used.

'Activity' methods are limited by the fact that the student is rarely required to reason deductively. Thus factory visits, films and banking 'kits' may well bring realism to the students' appreciation of some economic topics but that is not to say that they bring any comprehension of the real world. For example, if the child has no direct experience of a farm this is no barrier at all to understanding agricultural subsidies; of course, a visit by an urban child to a farm may well show the relevance of deductive reasoning to human problems but what it will not do is to bring analysis to human problems.

The economics teacher has twin responsibilities; he must teach economic analysis and then show its relevance to social problems because pupils easily conclude that it is nothing except an academic exercise. The first purpose can hardly ever be served by a visit or the use of visual aids; sometimes the second purpose can be fulfilled by a visit or a film which emphasizes the reality of economic topics. However, it remains true that these activities are quite insufficient in themselves in the training of economists and that their chief shortcoming is that though the students may be 'active' they need not be reasoning. To labour the obvious, this does not mean that they have no value at all.

N. Lee and H. Entwhistle take a comparable view to the use of analogies in verbal explanations:

> Insistence upon fidelity to the cake metaphor may seem fanciful and, no doubt, there are points at which it must be abandoned. But this sort of teaching by analogy is an important way of keeping theoretical teaching in touch with children's experience whilst, at the same time, extending their experience into areas where experience can only be, in the nature of things, a product of the imagination.[4]

Such teaching techniques as factory visits, films, 'dramatized' lessons or case-studies may be well suited for commerce courses and for general studies courses containing economics, but they are limited in their usefulness to the economic teacher concerned with systematic training in economic analysis. They must always be

---

[4] 'Economics Education and Educational Theory' in N. Lee (ed.), *Teaching Economics* (Economics Association, 1967), p. 46.

supplemented by oral questioning, discussion or instruction, and fit in well with the preceding and succeeding lessons.[5]

A case study The term 'case-study' is worthy of definition. It is sometimes used to mean no more than an extended example. For instance, a teacher concerned with the economic analysis of nationalized industries may use a detailed account of one industry to illuminate his account of, say, investment and pricing problems. All that need be said here is that this contains no special virtue but that it is fair enough as long as concentrating on one industry does not preclude particular formulations of these problems. This brings us to the crux of the matter. Such an approach looks as though it gives greater coherence by talking only of one industry, but it may in fact lose coherence because the student sees a particular example without necessarily realizing its specificity and without appreciating the characteristics of the general class to which it belongs. The appropriate attitude is that an extended example contains little of value per se, and it must not be judged against a more fragmented approach as though this was necessarily disparaged; it must be evaluated solely by the appropriateness of its example against that of alternative examples.

The term case-study is perhaps more properly used to mean, not an extended example, but a specially formulated example possibly based on real-world phenomena. In this case the example not only contains the characteristics in which the teacher is interested but it also poses a problem to the student. It might, for instance, provide him with a firm's demand and cost functions and ask him to recommend a pricing strategy for the firm.

The specified formulated case-study clearly differs from the instances of the extended example which analyses the recent history of a given firm or industry so that the student can practise his economic expertise on the past policies. The second sense of the term gives him the opportunity to practise that same expertise on future policies. Such a distinction may be important in arousing the students' interest but, once aroused, the relevant criteria is how well

[5] Details of these methods which can, of course, be quite valid within a given context can be found in R. H. Ryba, 'Teaching Methods and Aids – A Survey', and R. H. Ryba, 'An Economics Room', R. H. Ryba, 'Visual Aids', C. J. Sandford and M. S. Bradbury, 'Case studies in the Teaching of Economics', R. F. R. Phillips, 'Examples in Role-Playing', N. Lee, 'Visits and Field Studies' all in N. Lee (ed.), *Teaching Economics*.

the case-study calls on the students' analytic powers or helps him to deduce principles of general applicability.

It would be a sad irony to arouse interest and then dissipate the students' energy in inappropriate or trivial problems. Perhaps case-study techniques and the comments of Professor Sandford and M. S. Bradbury are especially worth mentioning. Both writers emphasize that their value is that

> ... they require the direct participation of the students, they are learning by doing ... the case study method carries the danger that one 'case' may be regarded as typical and generalizations may be drawn, based on a sample that is too small or too unrepresentative to warrant them.[6]

The most useful non-oral teaching method would seem to be the graph and the geometrical diagram. Both of these can show visually relationships between economic variables, perhaps between the employment level and investment, but what they do not do is prove anything since a diagram could be drawn showing a quite erroneous relationship between employment and investment. Students are rather apt to invest a diagram with explanatory powers

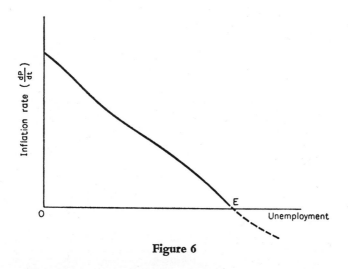

Figure 6

[6] 'Case studies in the Teaching of Economics', in N. Lee (ed.), *Teaching Economics* (Economics Association, 1967), p. 143.

that it does not really have. They may see a diagram on which the equilibrium level of national income is that level at which savings equals investment and then think that they know why that is so. The main purpose of the diagrams is as a memory aid and as a 'picture' of the relationships being studied.

A further convenient example is the Phillips relationship between the role of inflation shown on the Y axis and the magnitude of unemployment shown on the X axis in figure 6. This postulates high inflation at zero unemployment and no inflation at the unemployment level E and falling prices at yet higher levels of unemployment.

This diagram does not prove or explain anything; it simply asserts something. The teacher must be mindful that it is a convenient memory aid and nothing else at all since a quite different relationship could have been asserted – and that also would have been neither explained nor proved.

Both the damaging distortion and the helpful possibilities of diagrammatic teaching techniques are shown by the following example.[7] It is a diagram used in an explanation of the principle of comparative costs which was discussed in Chapter 2.

In figure 7, the production possibilities open to country A are shown on the axes corresponding to the origin OA. It can produce OYa of Y and no X or, alternatively, OXa of X and no Y or, yet again, any combination of the two goods on the line YaXa. In fact,

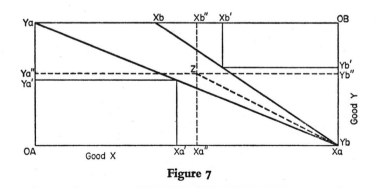

Figure 7

[7] See P. Kenen, *International Economics* (Prentice-Hall, 1967).

it chooses OYa', and OXa' on this line. Similarly, country B can choose any of the possibilities on YbXb and actually chooses the combination OYb' and OXb'. This is the situation before trade. In the course of international trade country A specializes in X and produces OXa while B specializes in Y and produces OYb. They then trade. The resultant position is shown at point Z where both countries have moved to combinations of the two goods previously outside the possibilities available to the two countries. Country A now has OYa″ of Y and OXa″ of X. Meanwhile, country B has OYb″ of Y and OXb″ of X. (In this diagram, A has foregone OXa″ – Xa of good X in order to obtain OYa″ of Y while country B has done the reverse although the amount of Y foregone is now expressed as Yb – OYb″, which equals OYa″, and the amount of X gained as OXb″ which, from A's viewpoint, equals the OXa″ – Oa foregone by A.)

Such a diagram has the undoubted advantage that the student can see the gain in world output and in the amounts consumed by each country. He cannot possibly deny that both countries are better off. The first difficulty is that international trade is not necessarily about gains in the quantities consumed of all goods; it is fundamentally about opportunity costs and only partly about gains in output and consumption. (It is true that the changed opportunity costs are shown by the slope of any line OXa to Z but only those students with a sound background in mathematics will appreciate this.)

A second important difficulty is that it deals with a very special case indeed. It postulates that each country is equally productive at one good, in this case good Y. Only by this felicitous assumption are the axes representing the output of both countries of good X of equal length and so the 'box' diagram produced. The theory of international trade also has to cope with models in which the countries produce unequal volumes of the goods.

A third difficulty is that, although the diagram shows that both countries are better off, it does little by itself to give the student any explanation of why this should be so.

Like most diagrams that give pictures of the results of some analysis, this one is insufficient as an explanation and a perfectly satisfactory lesson can be given without it. In other words, it is a teaching technique that is neither necessary nor sufficient in itself.

It must be said that it is a most deft diagram and that students appreciate it and, unless warned, read far too much into it. These forebodings are less true of some geometrical diagrams which can be used as a form of deductive reasoning.

It would be ingenuous to assume that pupils are geometricians, hence the only safe course is to combine oral exposition with diagrams and not to regard either as sufficient in itself. This will be true for most lessons. Nevertheless, the teacher must, where he can, ensure that his pupils are not playing a passive role. According to the subject and to the students' ability, the teacher must combine oral exposition, on his part, or by a member of his class (probably the single most important technique), reading by the pupils, problem solving by the pupils, such as the concentration policy mentioned above or the international trade example given in Chapter 2. These will provide his pupils with opportunities for active learning while extra-mural visits and most forms of visual aid will meet the educational needs of those pupils whose social awareness is inadequate. However, economists would not rank this latter point very high in their educative claims for their subject and such needs are best met by other subjects in the curriculum.

Let me finish this catalogue of abuse with a look at visual aids. I think the general principles must be clear enough. Devices such as overhead projectors, filmstrips or, best of all, wooden indifference curves, are most unlikely to lead to inductive/deductive reasoning although they may reinforce what has gone before or is to come.

These techniques are, at the best, trivial, and at the worst, quite bogus, and I might hope that I was stating the obvious and paying insufficient attention to such merit as they do have. But, judged by their publications, many people responsible for the professionalization of economics teaching are likely to trumpet the virtues and ignore the limitations. Mr Ryba holds that 'A portrait of Malthus might provide a starting point for a discussion of population problems'.[8] One hardly knows where to start. Just one point: If students were shown a picture of Nassau Senior and told it was Malthus they would understand neither more nor less about population. If a lie can be substituted for a truth and no damage done to understanding then there is something peculiarly redundant about that particular truth as a teaching device.

[8] Ibid., p. 181.

Many such examples of a bizarre overemphasis can be extracted from colleagues who have been on educational courses. It may be said of all these ways of departing from traditional lecture techniques that they arouse interest and, where true, that is in their favour. Since they may correspond very little to the true nature of economics we must often judge them as ways of arousing interest and on that criterion alone. It is difficult to see any analytic distinction between these methods of striking interest and, say, putting a live ferret down your trousers!

A further point to make is that, even if visual aids do arouse interest, is that what we are trying to maximize? It is a poor subject that only gains interest from the form of its presentation. In any event, 'interest' is a normative term; economics is, or is not, interesting to particular people and most people find some particular parts boring. A formal deduction is just that and we deceive the students by pretending that it is anything else. There is no reason at all to approach the teaching of economics as though we were doubtful of its intrinsic interest.

The economics teacher's attitude should be to use these techniques when they are appropriate and not to feel any obligation to use them.

Lastly, attention must be given to the language problems in economics teaching where resort is made to oral exposition. Here there are three separate problems. First, technical jargon such as the 'terms of trade' must be used where they carry an advantageous precision over the phrases used in popular discussion, and the difficulties of precise definition must not be shirked otherwise they create as many problems as they solve. Thus, 'Commodity Terms of Trade' must be distinguished from 'Factoral Terms of Trade' and they in their turn from 'Double Factoral Terms of Trade'. Second, there can be difficulties with ordinary words of non-technical nature. A term such as 'inflation' can have different meanings for pupils according to their family experiences or beliefs; thus for some it is an opportunity to gain a greater share of the National Income and for others quite the reverse. As economists they must abandon these value-loaded attitudes in favour of a technical approach, in just the same way that a doctor must regard a disease primarily as a scientific problem. Third, there are special problems for economists in that they have taken words in common use and given them different and peculiar meanings: the word 'rent' is an obvious example.

All these possible sources of ambiguity must be recognized and met by the most careful use of words and explicit mention of what the term does not mean. 'Normal profits', for instance, is another booby-trap. The economics teacher must spend much of his time expressly defining his terms and then consciously removing possible ambiguities.

It should be clear that the economics teacher, perhaps rather more than some of his colleagues in other disciplines, needs to spend time stating explicitly not only what he does mean but also what he does not mean. There are sufficient ambiguities and difficulties in economics without a teacher adding to them by careless misuse of words or by failing to draw attention to possible mistaken meanings that students might read into something. A teacher will find by experience where the most likely sources of confusion lie. Students often feel that profit maximization *implies* revenue maximization and it is worth the effort to demonstrate that this is not so by manoeuvring them into the sort of deductive process described in Chapter 2.

It is our central theme to examine the implications of the nature of economics for the teaching of the subject and, later, for its educational role. This chapter has demonstrated the way in which the nature of an economic explanation, and of an economist's jargon, generates problems for the economics teacher in the arrangement and communication of his material. It is, of course, true that many of these problems of organizing the material are common to most subjects; attention has been focused here on the way in which these problems manifest themselves in economics.

Some other viewpoints – a critique

It is worth devoting space to a short critique of some viewpoints quite different from those so far developed.

> ... it is advisable to give an outline of the subject straight away. ...
> The least satisfactory way of doing this is by the formal analysis of a
> textbook definition. The only place for this – if, indeed, it is needed at
> all – is at the end rather than the beginning of a course. At the start, the
> teacher needs an outline of the *content* of the course, and not of its

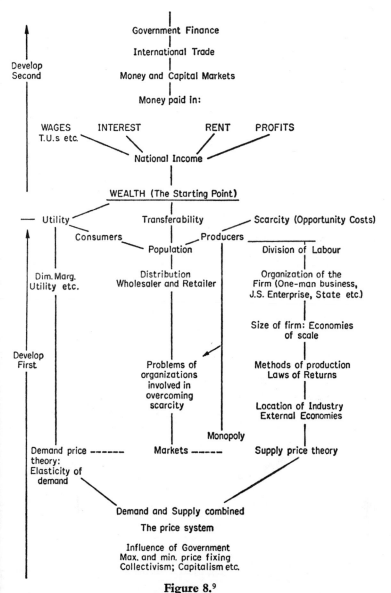

Figure 8. [9]

N.B.   This is fairly comprehensive and could be used in its full form only with mature students. It could be modified to suit other needs. None of the subject matter would be discussed in detail, the object being only to gain an overall picture of the problems involved.

[9] G. J. Edmunds, R. F. R. Phillips and R. H. Ryba (eds.) *The Teaching of Economics* (Economics Association, 1957), p. 31.

implications. A rather better method is by diagrammatic summary of which an example is afforded as . . . (figure 8).[10]

A preliminary comment is that presumably it is the student who needs an introduction! This quotation contains a number of remarkable assertions which are not deduced from stated hypotheses or assumptions. It is never shown what is inappropriate about a textbook definition nor why the student needs an outline of the content of economics.

It is implicit in this chapter and explicit in Chapter 2 that economics cannot be identified uniquely by reference to its content but only by reference to its methods and the problems to which they are applied. Thus the term 'joint stock enterprise' could occur in a law or politics syllabus and the deductive method occurs in subjects other than economics. The authors' misapprehensions are due to their failure to appreciate the importance of relating economics teaching to the nature of the subject. A student is thus best introduced to economics in the early lessons by learning of the methods used in economics and the problems to which they are applied. However, the most anomalous feature is Figure 8 itself.

It is seriously suggested that students should, in several lessons, be taken through this diagram by a Socratic question and answer method. It is claimed as an advantage that students 'should have the concepts of the circularity of Economics and of the main subjects and topics to be studied in detail later'. This seems an odd priority at such an early part of the course when initial interest can be generated and misunderstandings of what economics can, and cannot do, overcome. A consideration of the nature and limited applicability of deductive reasoning and of the necessity of inductive reasoning in applied economics can help to achieve this. It is doubtful whether this diagram could contribute anything in this way.

Furthermore, it is questionable whether the diagram achieves its object of presenting circularity for its construction seems arbitrary. It is difficult to see the validity of some of the suggested links; location of industry is hardly the first topic to come to mind in connection with the laws of returns. The diagram fails to emphasize the interdependence of economic concepts in that most concepts mentioned are shown as linking directly with only two other con-

[10] Ibid.

cepts but in fact many of these notions have important links with several topics. International trade, for instance, is important in any consideration of markets rather than of indirect significance as the diagram implies. Population could provide another example, and so on.

Another curious visual aid is the following diagram from the same pamphlet.

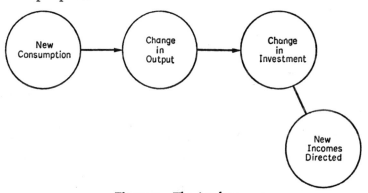

Figure 9. The Accelerator

This diagram is factually wrong if the identical areas of the circles is meant to imply that the money-value of the new consumption equals that of the new investment.

The figure is not self-sufficient and would need a complex verbal explanation so that at best it is a memory-aid and at worst, misleading. There are many aspects of the accelerator – such as the sources of the unequal changed values of investment and consumption – that this diagram does not begin to explain.

Other examples of unfortunate diagrams are available:

WEALTH

Individually owned		Collectively owned	
Personal possessions e.g. clothing	Business e.g. textile machinery	Capital e.g. coalmines	Collective possessions e.g. public library

The diagram[11] above contains the implication that coalmines are capital and that public libraries are not. It is an example of the awkwardness of imposing a *classification* – in this case by form of ownership – and mistaking the categorization for an *analysis*.

It is all too easy to be over-zealous about classification and to structure something which does not really have a structure. A less alarming example is our professional tendency to dichotomize consumption goods from capital goods and ignore, save at the advanced level, that many products, such as education, have both capital and consumption good characteristics. Of course, it is an easy and appealing classification for students beginning economics but it may sometimes separate into two classes goods which ought not to be separated even for these students. Nor is it entirely a frivolous example to observe that we may sometimes distort the significance of income and expenditure flows by allocating to yearly periods. It is not clear in what way it is important, in this connection, that the earth has just gone round the sun.

It is worth repeating the point that we modify the real world when we abstract general relationships and classify material and we must bear in mind the distinction between a modification and a distortion.

A catalogue of modifications which border on distortions might be teaching elasticity as a percentage ratio change instead of as a derivative, teaching credit multipliers as reflecting the real world, teaching 'the' multiplier as $\frac{1}{s}$ instead of a catalogue of multipliers, and so on. All these things occur and they are all attempts to be helpful and, at least potentially, they can all create more problems than they solve.

I have leaned hard on visual aids not because I think they have no value, for obviously they may be more legible than some people's handwriting, and prepared material for an overhead projector may well save classroom time. They have real practical values of this kind rather than as a substitute for conventional teaching. Unfortunately, my impression is that at this moment in time their limitations need to be clarified rather than their advantages because they have

[11] J. L. Hanson, *A Textbook of Economics* (Macdonald and Evans, 3rd ed. 1961), p. 25.

too many naïve supporters. And the same goes for case-studies, integrated sessions and so on.

When I come right down to it, I hope to live and die an old-fashioned 'sock-it-to-them' teacher. Excessive reliance on many modish techniques is for fools and zealots; I do not believe that many colleagues are fools and I, for one, am too old to be a zealot.

CHAPTER FOUR The Purposes of Economics Teaching

Most discussions of the claims, purposes and objectives of a syllabus are a curious mixture of the speculative and empirical. The present purpose is not to bring a Bloomian taxonomy to the role and claims of economics but to detail briefly some of the claims made for economics by its practitioners rather than by educationalists.

The provision of useful knowledge, facts or concepts, which economists believe to be served by their subject is true but too general.

It corresponds closely to the view of economics taken in the earlier chapters. Professor Stonier and Hague claim that:

> ... the value of economic theory lies in providing a framework of analysis which can be used by applied economists in interpreting facts about the real world.[1]

Of course, economists do not profess to interpret all the facts of the real world. The facts which they choose to interpret have been detailed in Chapter 2 and, put briefly, they are the implications for resource allocation of choosing between various ends.

The viewpoint of Professors Stonier and Hague is really a statement of the value of economic theory; this is not quite the same as a statement of the educational goals of teaching economics. It is a quite separate matter to show that the economist's interpretation of the facts of the real world has such an educational value that it

[1] A.W. Stonier and D. C. Hague, *A Textbook of Economic Analysis* (Longman, 1953), p. 498.

should be given to the pupils rather than, say, a geographer's interpretation of the real world. The problem needs to be posed in this way because the inclusion of economics in a curriculum must lead to the exclusion of something else. It must have an opportunity-cost.

Economists are also concerned with predicting and rigorously analysing the consequences of actions by individuals, firms and governments and thus clarifying the implications of the alternative courses of action which are open. Professor Lipsey makes the point in the following way:

> The economist fulfils a function by trying to get the final goals of policy stated as clearly as possible and seeing how the unsound and sound measures really do relate to these goals. In some cases, however, it is very difficult to discover if some circumstance is really desired as a final goal in itself or as a means to some other end. One example would be the external value of a country's currency (as shown by the Exchange Rate). Judging from their public statements, the great majority of British politicians believe that the value of the pound should be maintained at almost any cost. Faced with a choice between a constant Exchange Rate plus a constant standard of living and slowly depreciating Exchange Rate plus a slowly rising standard of living, some might choose the former. Now, if these people say that the prestige of the pound is so important to them 'per se' that they are prepared to sacrifice their living standards to maintain the external value of the pound, then this is a value-judgement and there is nothing in economics to say that people should not have such a scale of preferences. If, however, having chosen the first alternative, people then argue that the value of the pound had to be maintained because otherwise exports would fall and a whole series of calamities would ensue until our living standards were reduced, then it can be pointed out that the choice made was inconsistent with the desired objectives.[2]

The most obvious examples of this kind of work are in the field of government policy. The economic theory pertaining to these and other matters can be thought of in two ways. First, as a sort of mental filing system into which different problems can be conveniently fitted and, second, as a series of substantive empirical propositions. The relevant question to be asked with regard to this first way of looking at economic theory is its usefulness rather than rightness or wrongness.

[2] R. G. Lipsey, *An Introduction to Positive Economics* (Weidenfeld and Nicolson, 1963), p. 540.

Once economic theory becomes a set of substantive propositions economists attempt to be predictive. Thus, economists do their best to quantify the economic consequences of building the Victoria Line, of joining or not joining the European Common Market and so on. When the consequences are not capable of accurate quantification then the economist falls back, as best he may, on a *priori* reasoning.

A further educational goal claimed for economics is of a vocational nature. That is that the completion of an economics course will make some people better at their job than they would otherwise be, even though they may not actually be working as professional economists. They, too, are concerned with the problem of choice but this time within the firm rather than within the national economy. The general attitude taken is that some problems, which might appear to be problems for the accountant or for the engineer, are in fact economist's problems.

Speight makes it clear we can open out this claim for economics in the following way. For instance, the figures produced by cost accountants can be quite misleading if important decisions of choice are based upon them. A company, for example, might possess a machine which made for it components for its final product and these components could also be bought from some other firms. A typical decision would be whether to invest money in buying more of these machines or to invest money in some other activity. The cost accountant would value the output of the machine by imputing to this output an allocation of the total fixed cost of that machine, the cost of the raw materials used in production, the cost of man-hours involved in production and so on. If these costs were regarded as the value of the output to the firm then that firm might well misallocate investment to some other project rather than to further machines of this sort. The real worth to the firm of this machine is shown by the opportunity-cost; that is, by discovering what price the company would have to pay to buy its components from outside the firm or by discovering what price it could get by selling the output of this machine rather than by using that output itself. These are the real opportunity costs and it is possible for the price it would have to pay to another firm, or the price for which it could sell to another firm, to be quite different from the value of the resources it uses up in producing the component itself. A further example of this attitude that economics has a vocational usefulness to people working in firms is provided by Professor Baumol.

> The last few years have brought with them a happy increase in rapport between the Economic Theorists and the Management Economist. The development has involved their simultaneous realization that business practice can be a fertile source of more abstract analytical ideas and that the theorist's rigorous tools can make an important contribution to the analysis of applied problems.[3]

Which, if any, of these educational goals are relevant to the education of sixth-formers or college students not training as economists? If any of them are relevant, is economics the most effective way of meeting these goals? A preliminary point is, of course, that although other subjects can claim to meet these goals, economics can meet all of them at the same time, and this combination gives it a particular advantage.

Little can really be said about the first claim that centres on the idea that economics has some cultural value in providing useful knowledge. Such a claim does not provide a criterion of much operational value in selecting a curriculum for almost every other subject in the conventional curriculum could make similar claims. Most people would approve of the educational goal of stimulating 'life-long interest', and the provision of 'useful knowledge'. However, it hardly follows from this that economics should be taught to sixth-formers since if economics is taught, then some other subject is not taught and that subject might well have equal or better claims to meet this goal effectively. It is a problem of choice. To observe that economic problems are 'at the heart of modern society' is to drift into the banal for so are many other problems. No attempt seems to have been made to demonstrate that economics is better equipped to cope with these problems than any other social science or, for that matter, some course in civics or general knowledge. It is tempting to agree with Mr Speight that:

> . . . the odd hour or so a week [of economics] in the sixth form, as part of 'general education' is hardly worth the trouble.

[3] W. J. Baumol, *Economic Analysis and Operational Research* (Prentice-Hall, 2nd ed. 1965), p. 3.

Speight also remarks:

> ... we are all economists nowadays: any educated man who reads a quality newspaper carefully will achieve a fair degree of economic understanding by this means alone.[4]

It might seem that these general roles of background information can, for most sixth-formers, be met by putting newspapers in the library. To meet these goals by providing economics in the school curriculum is to invite a serious opportunity cost in the form of other subjects removed from the curriculum.

The second educational goal of economics is the more attractive. It concentrates on the fact that economics has intellectual rigour in the study of the allocation of scarce resources. As Speight says:

> ... economics is a proper study because it is intellectually respectable, that is, it can be made the vehicle of a strict intellectual discipline. This is for two reasons. First, because it involves looking at the world in a way which is, for most if not all of us, quite new. Economics is not primarily a body of knowledge; it is, as Keynes said, a method rather than a doctrine, an apparatus of the mind, a technique of thinking. To understand this method, to acquire this apparatus, this technique is difficult because it means building up new thought patterns. The kinds of economic concept which spring to mind in this connection are the idea of the margin and the equimarginal principle, the distinction between money and real things, the fallacy of aggregation, the economic concept of rent. Only in so far as it inculcates the techniques of thinking can a course of study be correctly described as a course in economics. Second, the study of economics imposes an intellectual discipline because if it is to be carried to any significant depth and breadth, the student must learn to handle a number of variables at the same time. Moreover, and this is what makes economics really difficult, there is usually some reciprocity between these variables.[5]

The general line of this argument then continues that students should be able to undertake economic analysis partly to contribute to the students' education because they will eventually be voters, and partly because they may one day be required to work as economists.

[4] H. Speight, 'Economics as a School Subject', *Economics*, vol. 5, pt. 4 (no. 20) Autumn 1964, p. 424.
[5] Ibid.

This seems to be saying that, whether they like it or not, people are in fact using economic concepts more or less daily. Once we acknowledge this development the problem becomes, not whether to focus people's attention on economic concepts but, given that it is already focused, to focus it properly. In other words, the case for the teaching of economics is not, in the main, that people should be interested in these topics but that they are already and to give them no formal training involves too great a risk.

At best this is a slippery argument and something of a non sequitur. A value-judgement that people 'ought' to do such and such is not a necessary implication from a statement of fact. It scarcely follows because students are, in fact, interested in economics that therefore they ought to study the subject. Students might, after all, be interested in perpetrating crime or vice. People who support economics teaching for the reasons discussed here are really engaged in the disguised value-judgement that economics is a worthy subject, and it is precisely this point which is difficult to establish although it is easy enough to assert. In practice these first two educational goals, that the subject has a cultural and an intellectual value, come to much the same thing. To say that economics can be the 'vehicle of a strict intellectual discipline' is surely to point to the particular way in which economics can contribute to a person's culture. That is the cultural value of economics manifests itself in the forms of useful knowledge and rigorous intellectual discipline. There may be a distinction between saying that a subject is cultural and saying that it is intellectual but it hardly seems important. Without violence to word-meanings all intellectual studies could be called cultural; the reverse is not, of course, always true.

If it is a respectable academic subject then this seems to provide an important educational goal, but the fact remains that to include economics in the sixth-form or any other curriculum for this reason must still involve an opportunity cost in the form of other subjects which are not taught to those particular pupils. These subjects, in their turn, are also seen by their teachers as serving certain educational goals and there is at the moment no way of quantifying the varying importance of these goals and thus ranking them. Any decision that economics should be brought into a curriculum at the expense of some other subject will remain a value-judgement. This may seem a heavy-handed approach to the obvious; the point is made in this way because many critics simply identify some values for economics and then conclude that therefore economics should be taught in sixth forms.

The third educational goal believed to be served by economics is the vocational one. It is a very plausible argument indeed to say that the studying of economics fulfils some direct vocational purpose for the students of, for example, business studies who can soon appreciate the overlap between economics and other subjects such as accounts. A very strong case can be made out for the teaching of economics in this context and also for the teaching of economics (or some other social science) to undergraduates in the natural sciences who may later be called upon to undertake economic decisions in some managerial position.

All this has little relevance to the traditional sixth-form curriculum. Economics could only be introduced into the sixth-form curriculum for vocational reasons if there were a radical change in the structure and philosophy of sixth-form education and clearly this problem is well outside the confines of this study. This is not, of course, to imply that all sixth-form subjects are non-vocational. There is a spectrum incorporating markedly vocational subjects (that have non-vocational values) such as physics, and scarcely vocational subjects such as geography. What makes it difficult to regard economics as a sixth-form vocational subject is that it is more or less necessary to study sixth-form physics to become a professional physicist but this is much less true in the case of economics. The universities (who have an effective monopoly of producing economists) used to be quite hostile to school economics and are still ambivalent in their attitude to it. Certainly it is in no sense necessary to study sixth-form economics to become an economist or even to gain some less specific vocational benefit from economics. This latter point holds since almost any vocational course in a subject like accountancy will contain economics within its own curriculum if economics is considered to have some general vocational benefit in that profession. The vocational aims of sixth-form economics then should be treated with scepticism and are of only secondary importance in justifying the inclusion of the subject in the sixth-form curriculum.

It seems, therefore, that the only educational functions which can really be fulfilled by economics in the sixth form are that it provides a rigorous intellectual training and that it copes with inescapable problems of the real world in the economy and the firm which otherwise may be severely mismanaged. The fact that it can provide a rigorous academic discipline is hardly a sufficient reason for including it in the curriculum. Other subjects, many of them traditional to the curriculum, can make equal or better claims in this respect. Even if economics can make a very good claim here, it is only a relevant point if there were evidence for the belief that rigorous intellectual study in one subject transfers its benefits to other aspects of life. Since this belief cannot be confidently sustained the claim that economics is an academically respectable subject has real impact only if it is coupled with the idea that the content of the subject is in some way important. Otherwise the rigorous academic training can be given by studying some other subject which does have direct relevance for the student.

On the whole, most people might find the case for economics teaching in the sixth-form to be strong just for this reason: it is an intellectually respectable subject and it addresses itself to problems relevant, directly and indirectly, to the student. However, this is not the end of the case for there are other questions to be answered before economics can be thought of as a school subject.

It could also be claimed that a distinctive contribution of economics to academic training is that a rational approach to experience will be distorted if it is entirely lacking in any social science training. This rationale holds that some people trained in the natural sciences do not apply the rigorous standards that they take for granted in their professional lives to problems that would benefit from this approach in the social sciences. Thus such people might assert that savings depend on interest rates, that devaluation is a disaster or that capital punishment deters murderers. These assertions may or may not be true; our present point is that many people who should know better never think of these propositions as testable. We might then feel that the teaching of a social science like economics in sixth forms carries the benefit that the students will apply a rational, rather than a superstitious, approach to social experience. This simply points to the form of the intellectual rigour available in economics and to its applicability.

Attention must now be paid to the problem of whether, given that sixth-formers should receive rigorous academic discipline, given that economic problems are self-evidently important to sixth-formers and that they are interested in them, the question still arises of whether that is sufficient reason for sixth-formers to be subjected to a course in economics recognizable as such by economists. It might be held, for instance, that these goals might just as well be met, or met more effectively, by the students following a traditional curriculum of rigorous academic discipline combined with a programme of general studies containing some economics. Economics could, of course, only serve effectively in this way as a 'minor' subject on the assumption that 'transfer of training' is a valid idea. Such an attitude would depend also on a rather different concept of the nature of economics to the one taken here.

It is one thing to identify the educational goals in economics and select from them the goals which are relevant to sixth-form education, but it is quite another thing to deduce that, therefore, economics should be taught to sixth-formers. It is a completely separate issue whether or not economics can fulfil these goals for sixth-formers or, for that matter, whether it is the best method of fulfilling these goals. In practice there is little agreement among the people concerned about how and whether economics can fulfil these goals for sixth-formers.

The situation is even more complex than the above might imply. Not only are economists disagreed about the content of the syllabuses suitable for sixth-formers but they are even disagreed about whether there is any syllabus that is appropriate for students in this age group.

At one end of the spectrum of opinion there is the hostility of Professor Lord Robbins to the teaching of economics in secondary schools at all. He feels that economics is too complex a subject to be appreciated by sixth-formers and that it also calls for a maturity of judgement which will normally be beyond them.

> No simple proposition in economics is likely to be true unless it is understood as being subject to a whole complex of assumptions, not likely to be read into it, save by those with both a sufficient knowledge of the system of propositions as a whole and of the world of reality to which they have reference.[6]

Many people agree with this view of economics but draw the

[6] Lord Robbins, 'The Teaching of Economics in Schools and Universities', *Economic Journal*, Vol. LXV, No. 260, December 1955, pp. 579–93.

opposite conclusion, and feel that it is for this very reason that economics is an appropriate subject for sixth-form education. The distinction between these two viewpoints might be put in the following way: either economics is unsuitable for sixth-formers because it is too sophisticated in its intellectual demands or, alternatively, it is appropriate for sixth-formers simply because it may well make them more sophisticated intellectually than they would otherwise be. The Council for Curriculum Reform takes the latter view:

> ... the very difficulties which in the past have been presumed to make economics and politics unsuitable as school subjects are those which, in fact, make them valuable.[7]

Opinions on these matters seem to fall into two main groups. First, there are those who feel that economics is quite inappropriate for sixth-formers not because it cannot fulfil educational goals, but because it is too difficult a subject to fulfil such goals for sixth-formers. The statistics on the growth of economics teaching show that this viewpoint, even if it is right, is having very little influence at present on the trend of events.

It might also be said that although Professor Lord Robbins is formally correct in drawing attention to the maturity of judgement required in economics and to its intellectual complexity it is doubtful if it calls for greater sensitivity of judgement than Advanced Level study of English Literature, or more mental gymnastics than Advanced Level mathematics.

A second viewpoint is that economics can fulfil educational functions for sixth-formers, although its proponents come from different ends of a spectrum. Some believe that economics is quite a simple subject and can be expressed in simple terms without in any way distorting the subject; others feel that it can fulfil educational goals for sixth-formers but that it is rather a difficult subject and that simplifications lead to serious distortion. The first three chapters of this book tend to the view that economics is quite complicated but that it can nevertheless be taught effectively provided that sufficient care is taken and certain principles followed. Those who hold this view, therefore, would teach economics in a relatively involved manner because they feel that it is the only way in which it can be of any educational value to sixth-formers.

[7] Council for Curriculum Reform, *The Content of Education*, 1965.

It is, of course, quite true that it is easy to find examples of the problems of allocation within the direct experience of the student. However, it is one thing to identify for him in an intelligible way various problems as being economic problems, but it is quite another to suppose that because it is easy to identify economic problems it is, therefore, easy to teach academic economics. It just does not follow that because the reality of economic problems can easily be *shown* by homely examples, then economics can be *taught* with the aid of homely examples. This kind of approach may well be helpful to the teacher and especially so when he is dealing with students at the start of their economics courses, but sooner or later, if the course is to be recognized as a systematic training in economics, the student must face the abstract analysis which is characteristic of the subject.

It may serve some educational purpose to talk about economic problems in a general way, but nothing is gained by pretending that such courses are a training in economics. Nor is anything gained by concluding that, because economic problems are easily recognized, therefore their analysis is also an easy matter. Physical pain is easily recognized but this does nothing to make medicine an easy subject. It does, of course, remain true that many economic problems are conveniently illustrated, and helpfully illustrated, by reference to problems within the experience of the student just as differential calculus may be taught by taking examples of the trajectory of a football rather than the traditional example of the trajectory of a cannonball.

This chapter is necessarily fragmented in nature. This is a manifestation of the fact that economists have no coherent attitude to the educational role of their subject and a discussion of it tends to have a 'bits and pieces' approach. This is not to claim that a chaotic statement merits a chaotic rebuttal but that there is no coherent view of the educational role of economics in the sense of a careful deductive argument; instead there is a series of more or less independent propositions which need to be treated separately. There is plenty of dissatisfaction with the present state of economics teaching in secondary schools. Not only do we have the opinion of Professor Lord Robbins, but there is also the attitude of Professor Lipsey:

> The experience of interviewing, for admission to the London School of Economics, students who have done 'A' Level Economics at School

makes it painfully obvious that from somewhere, I am never sure from where, students get such ideas as the ones that the Law of Comparative Advantage proves the Nations ought to specialize in the production of certain goods, that economics has proved that rent and price controls are wicked and ought not to be used. . . . Economic theory cannot, of course, ever show us what we ought to do, but only what will happen if we do certain things.[8]

However, this really amounts to a criticism of the present standard of economics teaching in secondary schools rather than a demonstration that by its very nature it is an unsuitable subject for sixth-formers.

It may be added that a further source of scepticism about the educational role of economics lies in a seemingly inescapable problem. The cleft stick takes the following form. It is easy to agree with Mr Speight that many students are already interested in economic problems without any training in the none-too-obvious techniques of economics. It is also easy to sympathize with the view of Keynes that many people are unknowingly placed in a strait-jacket of intellectual concepts. We are left with the problem that if students receive no training in economics, society may be guilty of allowing them to inherit grossly mistaken ideas but, on the other hand, if they are taught economics they may also be the victim of propaganda rather than economic analysis. Although it is convenient and correct to agree with Lipsey that economics cannot tell us what we ought to do but only what will happen if we follow some particular course of action, the implication for teachers is inconvenient in that – to be faithful to the nature of their subject – they have the difficult task of making Lipsey's point a central theme of their course. One is tempted to be cynical about whether this actually happens in sixth forms. In other words, economic problems are inseparable from value-judgements whether we teach economics or not. The fact that this is so is probably on balance a reason for teaching it and for teaching it very carefully indeed. As H. Ent-whistle says

If ever you undertook this view that teachers are not to be trusted there would be no curriculum for the schools to teach.

[8] R. G. Lipsey, *An Introduction to Positive Economics* (Weidenfeld & Nicolson, 1963), p. xiii.

And it follows from this that:

> The only sound education is that which mediates a grasp of principle. At the end of a century, when these children will only be middle aged, we will still want them to have some sort of economic understanding but by then, the form in which economic problems manifest themselves may be radically different from their characters today. . . . Hence, we do children no service educationally, if we merely describe contemporary problems and teach the answers to which the adult community is currently advancing for their solution.[9]

When economists claim that their subject is valuable because it provides background information, a deeper understanding of government policy issues and a useful expertise with which to confront real-world situations they make persuasive claims for their subject. But some people feel that these goals could just as well be met by courses in general studies which could hardly claim the title of economics but which would be less demanding on classroom time. Even if a systematic economics course might fulfil these goals much better, and many would feel that this is so, the fact remains that the case is unproven because it is unprovable. The effectiveness of different courses in serving different goals is unquantifiable and the priorities of different goals over one another are also unquantifiable so that the case for teaching economics in secondary schools remains a matter of opinion.

It remains a straightforward proposition that however else these goals might be met and whatever goals might rank above them in importance, economists claim on behalf of their subject that it is academically respectable, that it provides useful background information, that it gives a deeper understanding of specific problems both of the economy of the country and of the economy of firms.

We have discussed possible objectives of economics teaching largely in terms of sixth-formers as these are the largest single group of economics students in the United Kingdom. Clearly the list of goals would be altered for different courses. It would be both repetitious and boring to trace out such changes, some quite large, particularly as there are also variations between courses in general studies, HND and degree courses and so on.

[9] H. Entwistle, 'Educational Theory over the Teaching of Economics', *Economics*, vol. 6, pt. 4 (no. 24), Autumn 1966, p. 204.

CHAPTER FIVE   Problem-solving

For some while it has been fashionable to speak of a problem-solving approach to the teaching of economics. Without doubt this emphasis was overdue, and equally without doubt it promises more than it delivers. Put more cynically, the disciples and zealots that have espoused it have promised rather more than they have delivered. Problem-solving is seen both as a means and an end; this is rather unfortunate for a profession that is always making careful distinctions on just that point. Since one might as well be hung for a sheep as a lamb it is also claimed that problem-solving is an examination-technique to complement or supplant traditional essay answers. A rationale of problem-solving would probably adopt the following lines. First, a working definition. In a problem-solving approach the student is not primarily asked to write a discursive essay or recall definitions, but to resolve a problem that will yield an answer only if concepts particular to economics are put to careful use.

Our discussion cannot help but point up and refocus themes mentioned much earlier. Clearly the problem-solving approach, if properly executed, cannot help but correspond at least some of the time to the inductive aspects of economics. This is a welcome shift of balance from the earlier emphasis on deductive reasoning – sometimes to the exclusion of inductive problems. This has been particularly true of GCE economics but is also common elsewhere, except in the graduate business schools.

Just as a problem-solving motif corresponds to any proper recognition of the nature of economics so it also helps to break down arbitrary and harmful barriers between economics and subjects such as operational research, statistics and accounting. A third advantage relates to the goals of economics teaching. It is difficult to claim on the one hand that economics has both vocational value and a rigorous intellectual training to offer and then, on the other hand, to omit problem-solving from the education of an economist. Few employers are simply interested in essay-writers and most would like to be able to direct staff to a problem confident that they can recognize the correspondence between the problem and their own discipline.

An example may clarify this point. Students can be offered a problem in stages which might, in the first two parts, ask them to calculate profit-maximizing output from total revenue and total cost data, and then to recalculate after a change in local authority rates. The nub is, of course, that the answer is the same since such a charge is a fixed cost charge with no effect on marginal costs. Nevertheless, many students will solemnly recalculate all the marginal costs and revenues to yield the same answer. Yet others will get quite different answers!

What is really worrying is that many students reduced to a shambles by this question can write perfectly good essays on relating prices to marginal costs, bygones are bygones and so on. In other words, essay writing skill may mask the fact that a student cannot relate the principles he has been taught to an actual problem. It is not very different from being a gynaecologist who cannot deliver a baby. It is not to the credit of economics education that it has fallen into this trap. Many economics graduates can tell you all about investment appraisal but have never seen or used a discount table. No doubt our accounting colleagues have gone too far in the other direction but we must look at the mote in our own eye before casting out a quite different beam in somebody else's.

Further support for problem-solving lies in the preoccupation with a Kuhnian view of science as a mental apparatus for resolving problems. Clearly classicists and historians resolve problems though hardly with all this soul-searching narcissism. The point is that their problems can be expressed and solved in essay form; those facing the economist in government service or in business cannot always be expressed in that form. Many lead to a unique answer such as '7'.

To return to an earlier point, the ability to solve certain kinds of problems is a goal of economics teaching and, diligently constructed, the teaching or tuition device of problem-solving may meet that goal and others. It is always good to have it both ways. A further advantage is that making economic concepts operational adds interest to a subject for the benefit of those not attracted by the average textbook, while remaining faithful to the nature of the subject and without the vulgarity of visual aids.

It should be said clearly and carefully that there is as yet no evidence that this method improves examination scores compared to other teaching methods. This, of course, is evidence for an inductive attack on everything from problem-solving to examinations.

Considering the term problem-solving rather widely, there are at least four kinds of problems available. Some are multiple-choice like 1 and 2 below.

1. On December 24th, a florist has Christmas trees that cost 50p each which, if unsold, can be thrown away at no cost. If he is a profit-maximizer, should he:

(a) charge that price which maximizes profit from the trees sold?
(b) charge that price which will sell all the trees?
(c) charge that price which will maximize total revenue?
(d) charge 50p?

2. Old-age pensioners can enter a soccer ground for 5p instead of 25p. Total revenue rises. Does this imply:

(a) Aged persons have a greater price elasticity for soccer than other goods?
(b) Their price elasticity of demand for soccer is greater than that of the rest of the community?
(c) The increase in revenue from new supporters is greater than the loss in revenue from existing supporters?

Primarily, these are methods of assessment but they may help the teacher to detect misunderstandings not apparent from essays on the same topic and thus have an explicit tutorial role to serve.

It is perhaps worth sounding a cautionary note on the practical difficulties of using multiple-choice questions in the tutorial situation. Any experienced teacher has in his mind a 'bank' of oral or written questions on which he can draw more or less spontaneously, but the multiple-choice approach needs a lot more care. There is the requirement common to all questions that it should be able to rank candidates rather than that all or none should pass. The distractors must be unambiguously wrong without being so absurd that poor candidates can realize they are nonsense and obtain the correct answer by elimination even when they do not really understand the point. It is almost impossible for the teacher relying on native wit to match achievement to these aspirations. It is by no means self-evident whether a question meets these needs or not. There are fortunately a number of published books[1] on this kind of material which the authors have presumably tested on their own students so that even these do not correspond to the questions available to the examining boards which have been monitored on thousands of pre-test candidates.

A second group of problems are in the case-study form already discussed in Chapter 3.

Third, there are simulation problems which commonly require computer facilities. The difficulties here are of resource constraints rather than of principle.

The fourth kind are more immediately available and require concept manipulation in a real-world, or invented, problem that may generate a unique answer or a range of possibilities. Problems 3–7 are examples.

3.
$$D = 100-p$$
$$S = p-10$$

Find the equilibrium price and output before and after a tax of 20.

4. A firm produces two goods, x and y, with a limited amount of labour and machine time and warehouse capacity. Unit profit is 6 on x and 4 on y. There are 40 hrs. of labour time available and each unit of x needs 2 hrs. and of y needs 4. The machines can run for only 28 hrs. X needs 2 hrs. and y needs 1. Storage space is 32 sq. ft, both x and y need 2 sq. ft. per unit. There is a regular contract to produce 10 units of x.

Find the profit maximizing output-mix.

[1] An excellent example is G. F. Stanlake, *Objective Tests in Advanced Level Economics* (Longman, 1969).

5.

Q	TC (000s)	TR (000s) per week
4	40	88
5	60	108
6	75	120
7	85	133
8	90	144
9	100	144
10	115	138
11	135	121
12	160	108

Find the profit maximizing output.

Find the effect on price and output of a change in local authority rates of £4 000.

Suppose, in the initial situation, the firm is offered £100 000 to produce 5 per week and that any other quantity can then be sold on the open market. Should the firm take the contract? How much would it then sell on the open market at what price?

Problem three emphasizes – for those students able to benefit – that demand and supply 'curves' are really graphical representations of simultaneous equations and that is their 'nature'. The familiar diagrams are really pictures. It also leads easily to the situation in which a tax increase is not wholly reflected in the price increase and thus raises the problem of incidence.

Problem four is a straightforward linear programming problem and, in those courses where it is appropriate, it should occur as naturally and rightfully in the economics course as in a quantitative techniques course. These OR methods are particularly useful in a problem-solving approach as they can be used to tighten up the economic theory clarifying its importance. A good example is the way in which the shadow prices generated in an L.P. solution identify the opportunity, or marginal, costs of production. It is all too easy for the traditional textbook accounts of market structures to give the impression that the case of monopoly price exceeding marginal cost is a geometric curiosity.

Problem five is a poor examination question at the GCE level because it fails to discriminate the good from the bad. Students who can write good essays about bygones are bygones and the irrelevance of fixed cost changes to marginal costs fail to see the correspondence with this kind of numerical case. It is, therefore, an excellent tutorial question; furthermore its arithmetic form is realistic compared to the smooth continuous profit-maximizing graphs of the average textbook.

6. A company produces 200 000 suits a year for wholesalers in 9 months each year with January–March 90 per cent idle during which maintenance etc., is carried out. They are offered a contract to produce 50 000 suits, to be delivered in the first two months of April if the price is less than £30.

The internal decision is to refuse because:

Labour	£14·00
Material	13·50
Depreciation	1·48
Overheads	2·13
Administration	1·15
Repairs *et al.*	1·92
Total cost per suit	£34·18
10% mark-up	3·42
	£37·60

A consultant advises:

Direct labour	£11·90
Material	12·90
Spoilage	£00·60
Total direct costs	£25·40
Indirect labour	3·00
General factory	2·20
Depreciation	1·80
Repairs, supplies, administration	2·68
	£35·08

Also overtime would be necessary at 20 per cent of direct labour, extra supplies necessary from a new supplier who refused usual 2 per cent discount. The consultant's fee was £2 000.

(a) Should the company sue the consultant?
(b) Should the company take the contract?
(c) In what circumstances would you reverse your decision on (b)?

Problem six is really only suitable for an economics syllabus within a business studies context because of its call for some elementary accounting. It contains a number of ingenious pitfalls and leads to lively class discussion.

7. *Cost-benefit Analysis*
Downtown parking authority – a municipal parking facility:

At a meeting in the Mayor's Office, the Parking Administrator proposes a new multi-level parking garage in Elm Street. The land is owned by the city and has a fire-gutted cinema with an expired lease. Demolition would cost £40 000. A builder has tendered £2m. to build an 800-space garage with a life of 40 years. The city can issue 20-year bonds at 5 per cent redemption commencing after three years with one-seventeenth being redeemed each year thereafter. A parking management firm will operate the garage for £30 000 p.a. Estimated costs are £240 000 p.a. Any revenues in excess of £270 000 to be split 90/10 between city and firm. Any deficit below £270 000 to be borne by the city. The ground floor can be let retail for £50 000 p.a. There is a private 400-space garage three blocks away charging 75p. for the first hour, 50p. for the second, and then 25p. with a maximum charge of £2. It is 75 per cent full with all-day parkers and daily there are another 400 cars staying for about 3 hours. Saturdays it is 75 per cent full of 2-hour parkers until 6 p.m. and then full from 8 p.m. until midnight. Sundays are quiet but it is 60 per cent utilized from 6 p.m. till midnight. Each weekday 50 000 cars enter the Central Business District and there is a demand for 29 000–30 000 spaces in this CBD. There are currently 22 000 spaces, 5 per cent metered with 2-hour maximum at 20p., 65 per cent are in open lots and 30 per cent in private garages. 60 per cent of all auto passengers entering the CBD are commuting, 20 per cent are shopping and 20 per cent businessmen making calls. The Elm Street site is central to the CBD, five blocks from a freeway access ramp and three from a new municipal music theatre. The *Finance Director* objects that the Elm Street site could be sold to an office developer for £1m. and the city would get £200 000 p.a. in property taxes. The office would include an underground garage so improving the tax base, city revenues and parking space at no cost to the city. An office building would improve amenities. The *City Planner* feels that a multi-level parking garage will increase more intensive use of shops, offices, etc., so raising land values. The underground garage would be used solely by the office users and would do nothing for total supply. Long-term parking should be discouraged to counteract suburban growth. The existing neighbourhood garage clearly favours long-term parking; the rate structure in any garage of ours should favour short-term parking. Commuters should use the mass transit system.

The *Finance Director* points out that the city subways are running below capacity and at a deficit. Why build a new city garage three blocks from the new subway station at the new music theatre and encourage further subway deficit. Each car driver means an average fare loss of 50p. to the subway system. About two-thirds of all CBD travellers have to come anyway even if they cannot bring their cars.

The *Mayor* says that people prefer to drive and do not like carrying shopping bags. The Downtown Chamber of Commerce has told him that each new parking space generates £10 000 extra in retail sales p.a. Retail profits are 3 per cent of gross sales after tax and the city gets 3 per cent sales tax.

The *City Planner* observes that there are other costs of parking, extra city street maintenance, congestion costs, etc.

What should be the Parking Administrator's reply?
If they do build, what should be their prices?
What other information do they need?
What should the Chamber of Commerce be prepared to pay in kickback to the Mayor?

In the majority of these cases the student will have to put to some operational use concepts and techniques he has already learnt; rather like a medical student going from discussions of optimal extraction to actually taking out an appendix – presumably from a dead body if we are to find some correspondence with the absence of real-world implications if the economics student makes a mistake.

A greater emphasis on this kind of work rather than the more traditional essay and discussion type of tutorial (they are comple-ments and not substitutes) yields the advantage that such a student could be of some use to an employer rather sooner than the tradi-tional type of economist. Secondly – and I think more important –

by forcing him to use the ideas he is more likely to have a better understanding.

As well as any pedagogic advantages, there are syllabus and curriculum implications. The traditional division between economics, operations research, statistics etc. becomes redundant. We could simply think of the courses as economics 1, 2 and 3. It would also lead us to embrace the more respectable parts of accounting. To repeat the motif – we would do well to redefine the boundaries of economics.

I am not here advocating a philistine replacement of theory by so-called 'applied'. There is no such trade-off and that misconceives our choice. I am talking of complements, not substitutes. I am talking of drawing out the operational significance of economics. In that event, we could be quite sure that Kafka was not thinking of us when he wrote, 'All these parables set out to say merely that the incomprehensible is incomprehensible and we know that already. But the cares that we have to struggle with every day, that is a different matter.'

That would not be a wholly unfair comment on the Hague–Ferguson–Braff syndrome or at least a reliance on solely that kind of economics.

I should like to claim that this is of general applicability. We must be wary of attempts to modify our subject to make it palatable to poor students or to fit into a course that can only allow of economics 1. There are plenty of precedents in which the expansion of a profession is also its dilution. And much of the best economics is available for many students.

> The basic ideas that lie at the heart of all science and mathematics are basic themes that give form to life and literature are as simple as they are powerful.[2]

[2] R. G. Lipsey, *An Introduction to Positive Economics* (Weidenfeld & Nicolson, 1st ed. 1963), p. xiv.

A Select Bibliography on the Teaching of Economics

Nature of Economics

Friedman, M., 'Methodology of Positive Economics' in his *Essays in Positive Economics* (Chicago University Press, 1963).

Klappholz, K. and Aggassi, J., 'Methodological Prescriptions in Economics' in *Readings in Micro-economics*, D. Kamerschen ed. (World Publishing Co., 1967).

Kuhn, T. S., *The Structure of Scientific Revolutions* (Chicago University Press, 1970).

Lange, O., 'The Scope and Method of Economics' in *Readings in Micro-economics*, ibid.

Lipsey, R. G., 'Positive Economics in Relation to some current trends', Vol 5, Part 3, No. 9, Spring 1964.

Robbins, Lord, *The Nature and Significance of Economic Science* (Macmillan, 1952).

Teaching problems

AMA, *The Teaching of Secondary School Economics* (Cambridge University Press, 1971).

Attiyeh, R. and Lumsden, K. G., 'University Students' Initial Understanding of Economics', *Economica*, New Series, Vol. 38, No. 149, February 1971.

Carr-Saunders, Sir A. M., 'The Place of Economics and Allied Subjects in the Curriculum', *Economic Journal*, Vol. LXVIII, No. 271, September 1958.

Council for Curriculum Reform, *Content of Education*, 1965.

Fowler, P. S., Ryba, R. H. and Szreter, R., *An Annotated Bibliography of Economics Education 1945-71* (Economics Association, 1972). This offers a comprehensive coverage.

Knopf, K. and Stauss, J. H., *The Teaching of Elementary Economics* (Holt, Rinehart & Winston, 1965).

Lee, N., (ed.), *Teaching Economics* (Economics Association, 1967).

Lumsden, K. G., *New Developments in the Teaching of Economics* (Prentice-Hall, 1965).

Lumsden, K. G. and Attiyeh, R., *Recent Researches in Economics Education* (Prentice-Hall, 1968).

Speight, H., 'Economics as a School Subject', *Economics*, vol. 5, pt. 4 (no. 20) Autumn, 1964.

Robbins, Lord, 'The Teaching of Economics in Schools and Universities', *Economic Journal*, Vol. LXV, No. 260, December 1955.

Index